AF413340

Pablo Picasso

Boy Leading a Horse

ANNEMARIE IKER

THE MUSEUM OF MODERN ART, NEW YORK

Pablo Picasso (Spanish 1881–1973). *Boy Leading a Horse.* Paris, 1905–06. Oil on canvas, 7' 2 ⅞" × 51 ⅝" (220.6 × 131.2 cm). THE MUSEUM OF MODERN ART, NEW YORK. THE WILLIAM S. PALEY COLLECTION

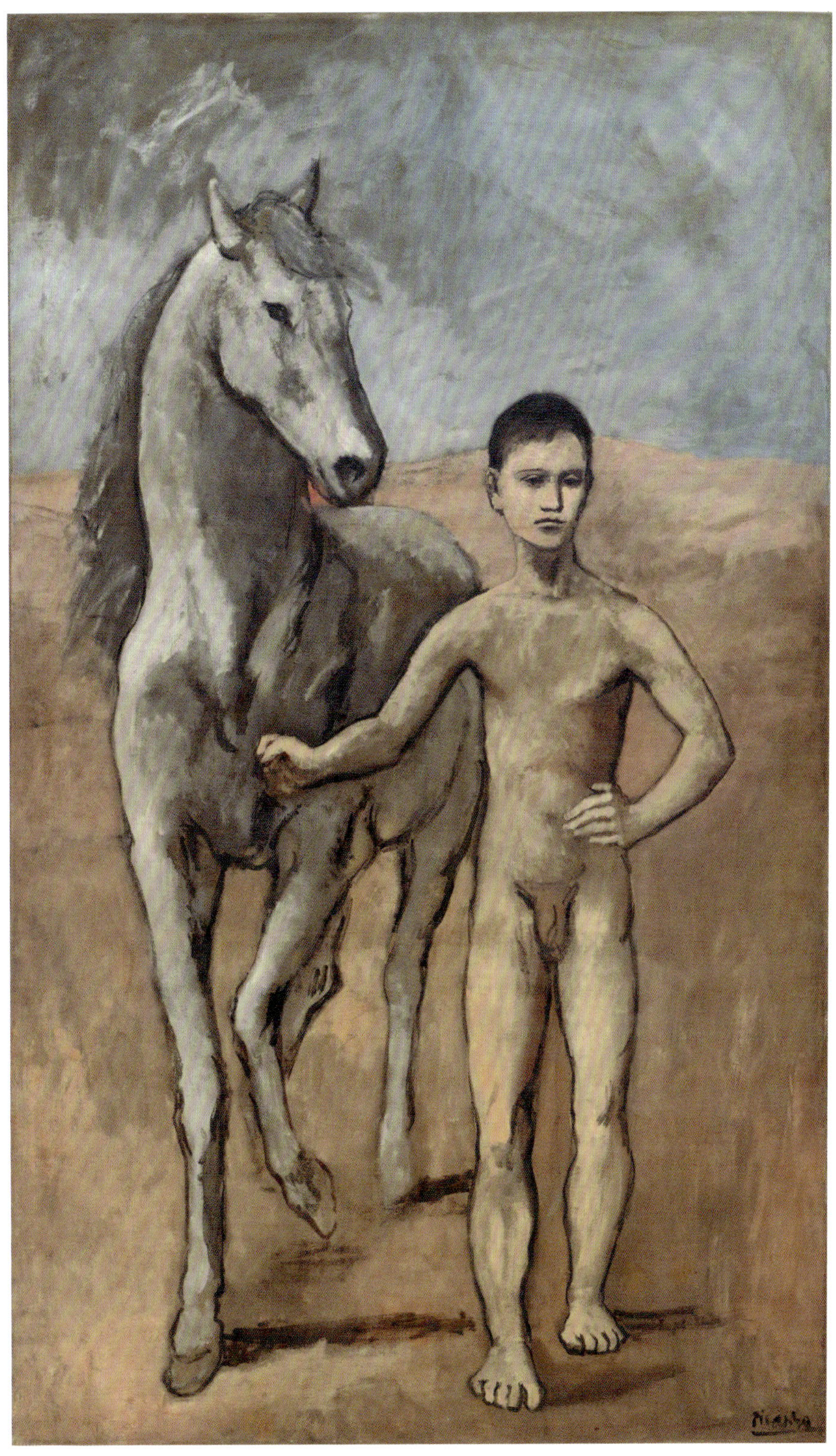

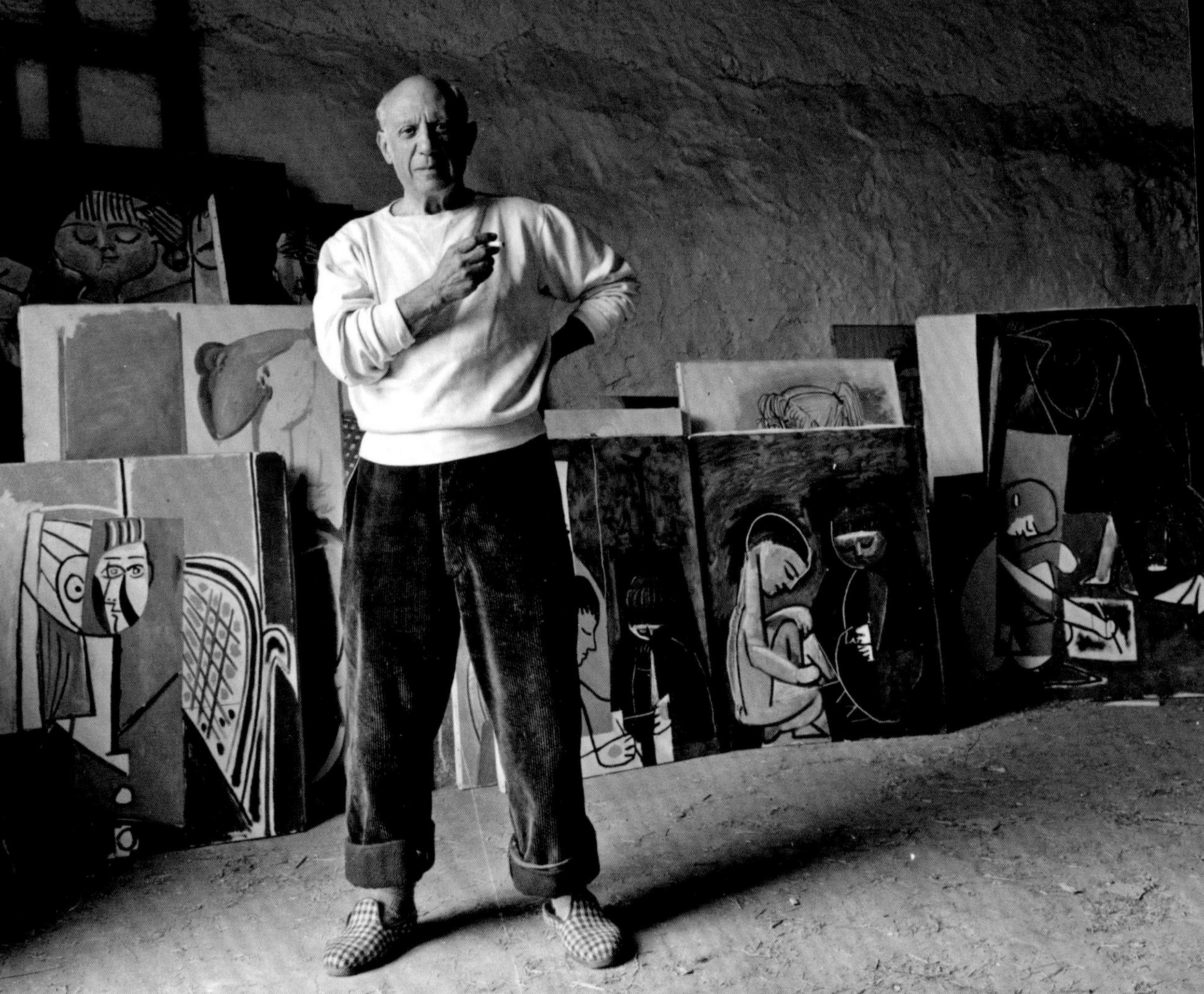

So asked Alfred H. Barr Jr., the founding director of The Museum of Modern Art, in the first sentence of *Picasso: Fifty Years of His Art*, published in 1946.[1] The artist, who was then sixty-five, had already been the focus of hundreds of books (and articles): critical treatises, scholarly monographs, and exhibition catalogues, along with biographies, memoirs, interviews, even poems. What more was there to say about him?

Plenty, said Barr. In his opinion, Pablo Picasso and modern art were synonymous **[FIG. 1]**. For Barr, no artist was more discussed during the twentieth century, and no artist was more engaged with the broad range of subjects and styles present in twentieth-century painting, sculpture, drawing, and printmaking. With *Picasso: Fifty Years of His Art*, Barr wished to provide a comprehensive survey of the artist's works—in particular, his early works **[FIGS. 2, 3]**, which had shocked viewers with their radical approaches to line and form, space and color, figures and facture. Equally shocking, in those early works, was the pace at which Picasso was experimenting with new artistic sources, techniques, and strategies. "Between 1905 and 1915," Barr declared, "the sequence of changes in his art often constitutes milestones, even monuments, along the highroad of Western art."[2]

One such "milestone," one such "monument," was *Boy Leading a Horse*. The twenty-four-year-old Picasso conceived the painting toward the end of 1905, after moving from Spain to France the previous spring in search of professional opportunities and connections. In Paris, where he had settled, he established formative relationships with artists, writers, dealers, and collectors. He had also

FIG. 1. Arnold Newman (American, 1918–2006). *Pablo Picasso*. 1954. Gelatin silver print, 12 7/16 × 10 1/16" (31.6 × 25.5 cm). THE MUSEUM OF MODERN ART, NEW YORK. GIFT OF GARY DAVIS

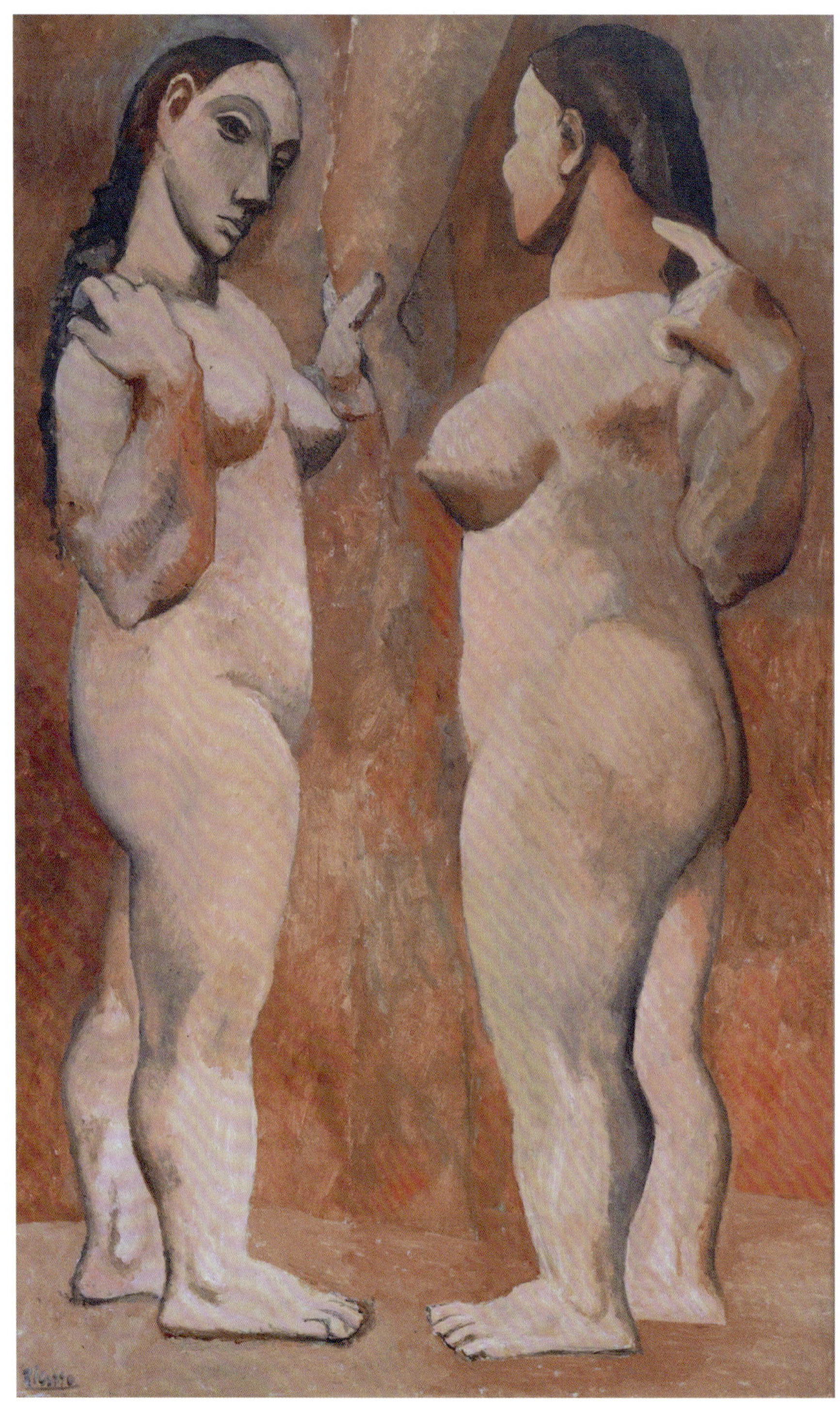

FIG. 2. Pablo Picasso (Spanish, 1881–1973). *Two Nudes*. Paris, late 1906. Oil on canvas, 59 ⅝ × 36 ⅝″ (151.3 × 93 cm). THE MUSEUM OF MODERN ART, NEW YORK. GIFT OF G. DAVID THOMPSON IN HONOR OF ALFRED H. BARR, JR.

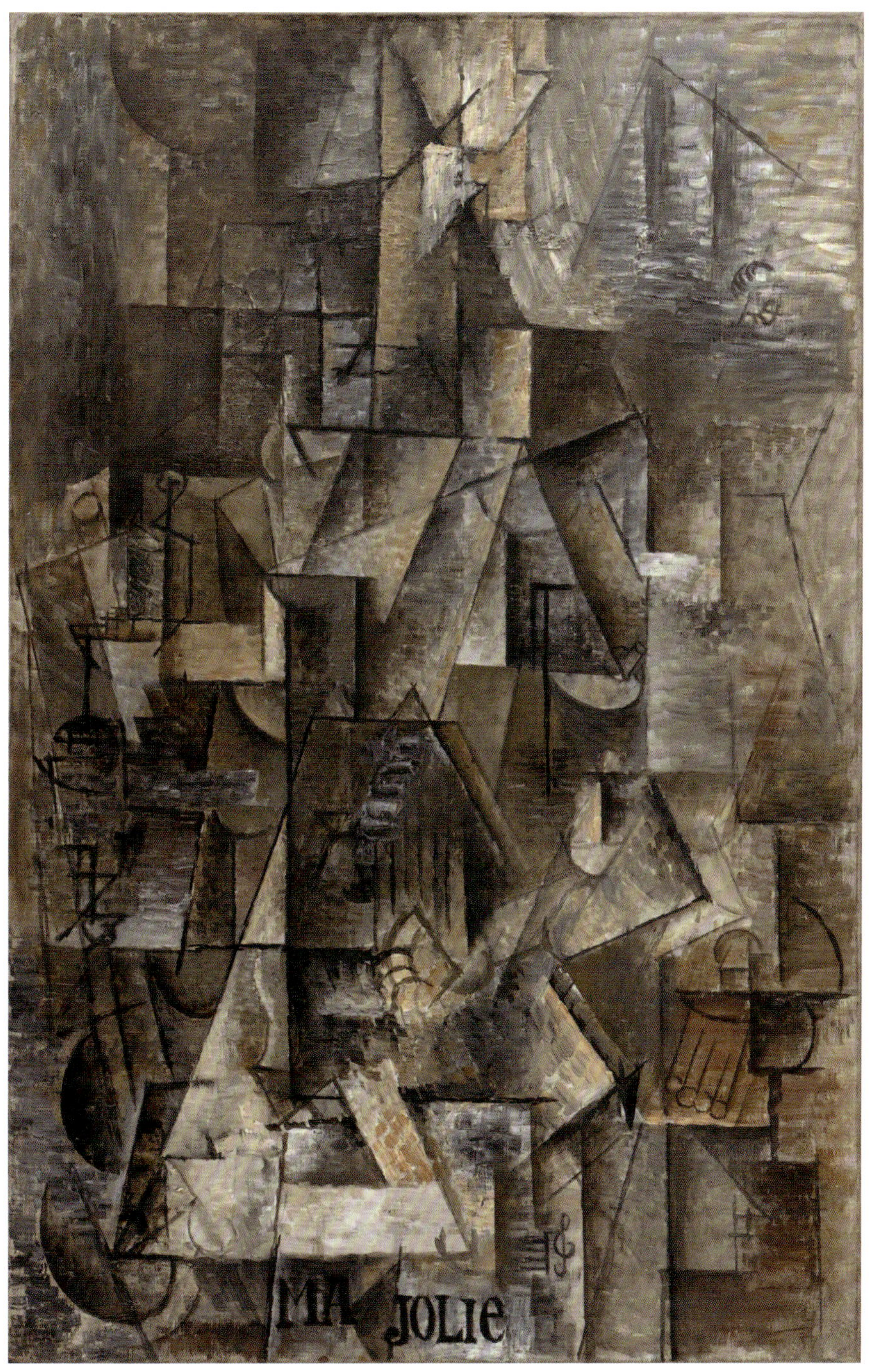

FIG. 3. Pablo Picasso (Spanish, 1881–1973). *"Ma Jolie."* Paris, winter 1911–12. Oil on canvas, 39 ⅜ × 25 ¾" (100 × 64.5 cm). THE MUSEUM OF MODERN ART, NEW YORK. ACQUIRED THROUGH THE LILLIE P. BLISS BEQUEST (BY EXCHANGE)

transformed his art, shifting from the bleak themes and hues that defined his Blue Period (from 1901 to 1904) to the lighter, brighter ones that characterized his Rose Period (from 1904 to 1906). About those years, the critic Gustave Coquiot explained that "Picasso is still finding himself." (It was Coquiot who first classified the artist's early works into distinct periods.) "He keeps on attempting the impossible, and he goes down each and every road."[3]

By late 1905 Picasso was approaching the end of one road and the beginning of another. Behind him was his Blue Period; ahead of him was *Les Demoiselles d'Avignon* [FIG. 4], which would scandalize the art world with its abstracted depiction of five sharp-edged, stylistically disjointed female nudes. "During this brief moment in his youth," Barr wrote, Picasso "was able to hold in delicate, intuitive balance the human and the ideal, the personal and the traditional."[4] *Boy Leading a Horse* emerged from this phase of private introspection and art-historical investigation. What did it mean to be a modern artist at the start of the twentieth century—an age of profound social, economic, and technological change? How should modern artists engage with these changes in their art? And how should modern artists engage with their artist precursors and contemporaries, both those they emulated and those they rivaled? Picasso likely contemplated these questions while at work on the monumental, mysterious *Boy Leading a Horse*, which some scholars have interpreted as a meditation on art making itself. This volume—"another book on Picasso"—examines the creation of the painting and its place at a major juncture in the artist's career.

———

In 1947 the art collector and critic Leo Stein pronounced *Boy Leading a Horse* "one of the best things of the period."[5] By "period," he meant the years around 1900, when artists such as Paul Cézanne, Henri Matisse, and Picasso—the youngest of the three—were upending traditional expectations about the look, making, and meaning of artworks. Works by these artists formed the core of the celebrated collection assembled by Leo and his sister, the writer Gertrude Stein, during the early twentieth century [FIG. 5]. Displayed on the walls of their shared studio in Paris, this collection astonished visitors. "Some came to mock and remained to pray," Leo wrote of the lively Saturday-evening gatherings that he hosted with his sister.[6] Together, the siblings brought about many a conversion to modern art.

The Steins were the first private owners of *Boy Leading a Horse*, which they acquired from the Paris-based art dealer Ambroise Vollard in 1906 or 1907. Until 1913 or 1914, the painting hung in their Paris studio in the prominent position shown in a photograph of the studio's east and south walls taken around 1907 [FIG. 6]. Stretching from the top of a paneled armoire to the lofty double-height ceiling, *Boy Leading a Horse* is immense and imposing—larger by far than the paintings on view around it. Sheer size, though, is not the only factor that made it stand out in

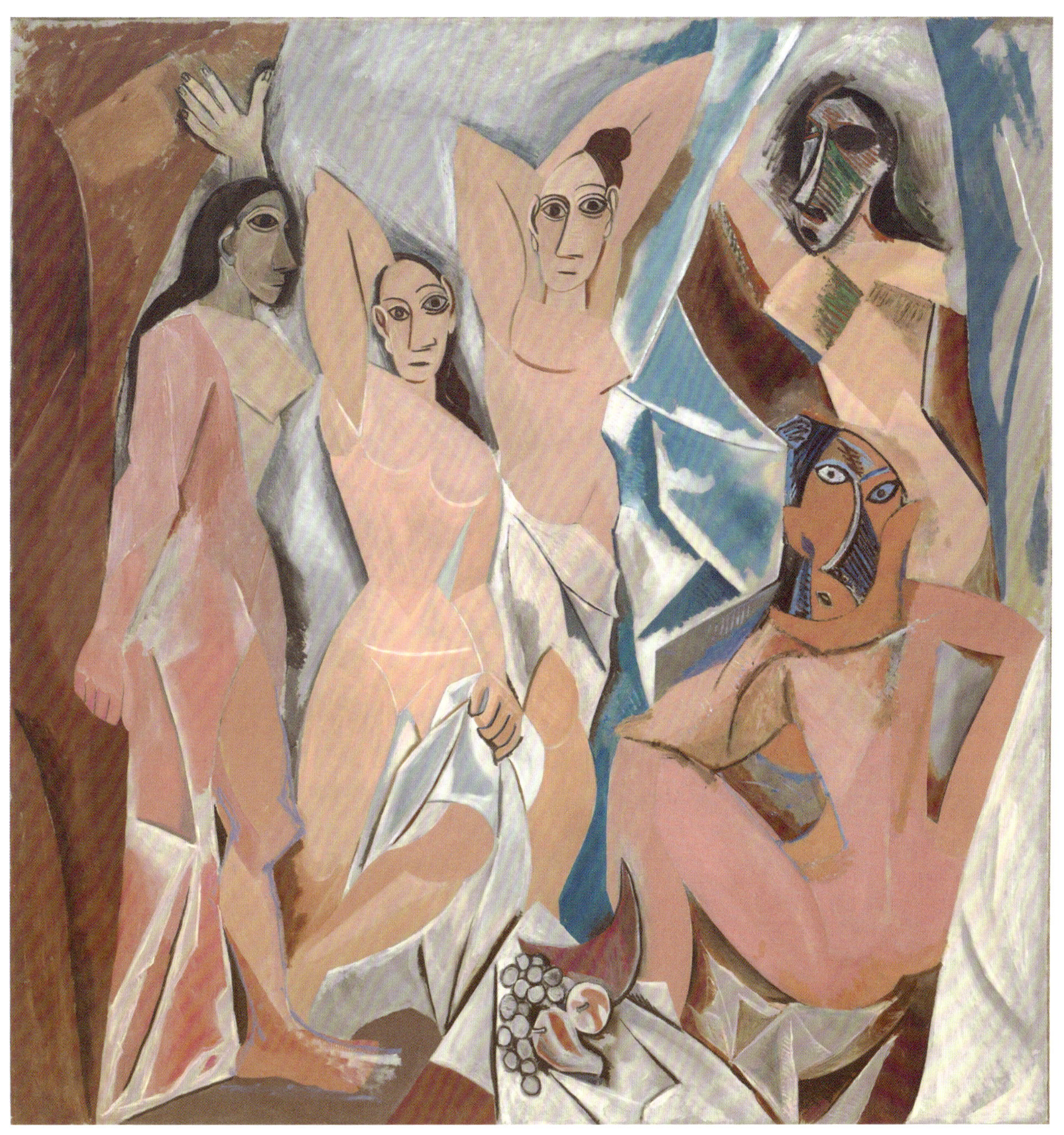

FIG. 4. Pablo Picasso (Spanish, 1881–1973). *Les Demoiselles d'Avignon*. Paris, June–July 1907. Oil on canvas, 8′ × 7′ 8″ (243.9 × 233.7 cm). THE MUSEUM OF MODERN ART, NEW YORK. ACQUIRED THROUGH THE LILLIE P. BLISS BEQUEST (BY EXCHANGE)

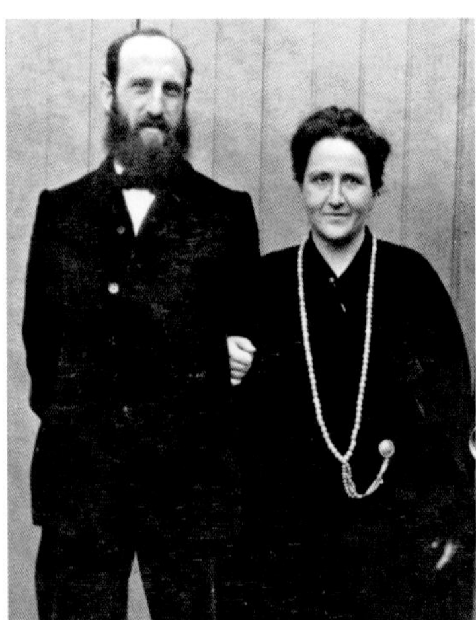

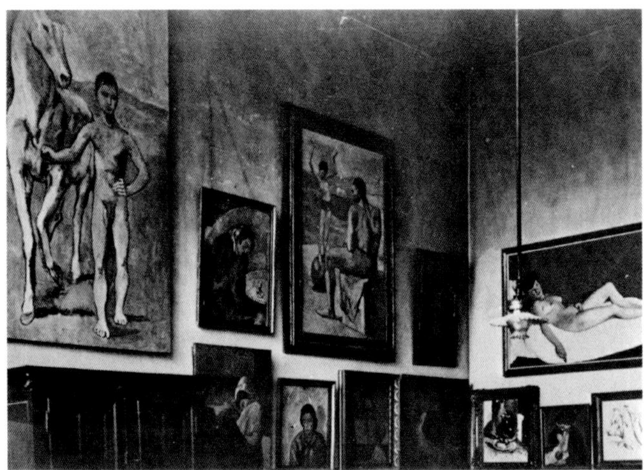

FIG. 5. Leo and Gertrude Stein, Paris, c. 1906

FIG. 6. "Studio of Leo and Gertrude Stein, 27 Rue de Fleurus, Paris. About 1907," in *Four Americans in Paris: The Collections of Gertrude Stein and Her Family* (New York: The Museum of Modern Art, 1970)

the Steins' studio. The painting's vigorous brushwork and stark palette set it apart from others nearby. So, too, did its figures: The boy and horse of the title all but fill the frame, their trim yet muscular builds defined by dark outlines and deep shading. Stepping forward, both project a steely firmness of mind, body, and purpose.

Yet what this purpose might be remains obscure. *Boy Leading a Horse* appears detached from time and place—specifically from early twentieth-century Paris, the time and place of its making. The painting's protagonists move through a desolate landscape of low hills, empty of human-built structures, under a leaden sky, the boy with no clothing and the horse with no saddle, bridle, halter, or reins. Both figures cast short, stubby shadows at their feet despite the absence of an overhead light source. Alone except for each other in an unidentifiable setting that The Museum of Modern Art curator William Rubin described as "a kind of nonenvironment," the boy and horse seem isolated from their surroundings, largely because of their thick contours, stiff postures, and stony expressions.[7] Although they stand on the threshold of the picture—with one more step, they would leave it altogether—they appear as distant, psychologically speaking, as the undulating horizon line behind them.

The Steins displayed *Boy Leading a Horse* near *Young Acrobat on a Ball* [**FIG. 7**], another Picasso painting in their collection. As in *Boy Leading a Horse*, an otherworldly air pervades this circus scene set in a parched, featureless landscape. In the foreground, a burly athlete watches a slender young acrobat practicing her balancing act. The athlete, seated on a cube, is wide and sturdy, with rippling muscles that push through his leotard, while the androgynous acrobat, poised on a sphere, is narrow and willowy, her waist no bigger than the athlete's

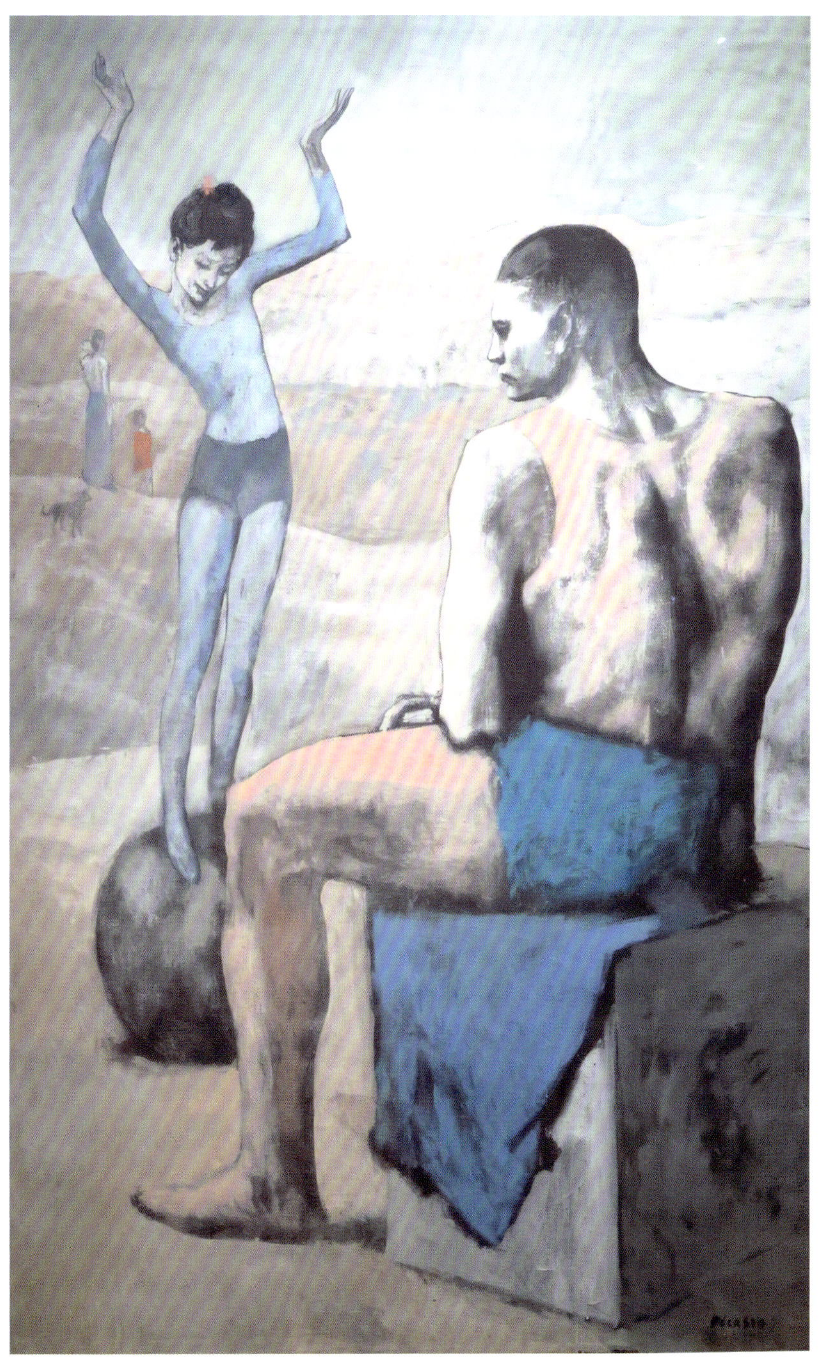

FIG. 7. Pablo Picasso (Spanish, 1881–1973). *Young Acrobat on a Ball*. Paris, 1905. Oil on canvas, 57 ⅝ × 37 ⅜″ (146.4 × 94.9 cm). PUSHKIN STATE MUSEUM OF FINE ARTS, MOSCOW

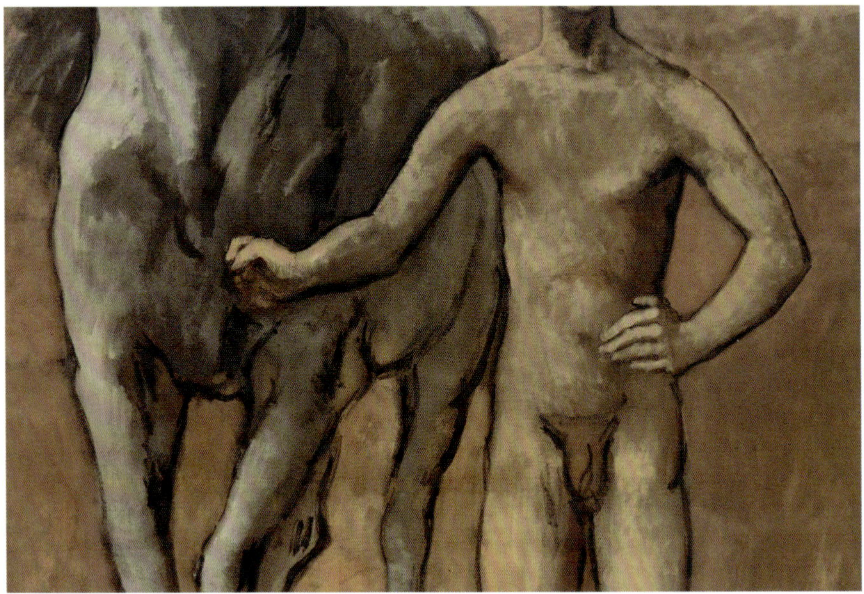

FIG. 8. Pablo Picasso (Spanish, 1881–1973). *Boy Leading a Horse* (detail). Paris, 1905–06

thigh. Behind them, a woman with a baby on her hip and a child by her side looks toward a white horse grazing on a nearby ridge.

According to the art historian Meyer Schapiro, the true subject of *Young Acrobat on a Ball* is "the artist figure, the performer, as triumphant."[8] Like performers, artists use their bodies and minds to captivate viewers; also like performers, they hone their skills through arduous practice. For these reasons, Schapiro concludes, *Young Acrobat on a Ball* represents the "consciousness of art as a skilled activity."[9] Comparable claims have been made about *Boy Leading a Horse*. The boy, similar to the balancing acrobat, performs a "skilled activity"— in this case, guiding a horse. Yet the way in which he performs this skilled activity merits scrutiny. On first glance, it looks as though the boy is using reins to steer the horse. (Indeed, viewers may initially "see" the reins they expect to see.) But on second glance, their absence becomes apparent. Instead, the boy controls the horse using only his outstretched arm and empty fist [FIG. 8].

This enigmatic gesture has intrigued viewers for decades, inviting an array of interpretations.[10] For the MoMA curator Kirk Varnedoe, it indicates the boy's mental—as opposed to physical—power. "In the way Picasso uses the gesture here," he wrote, "the notion of mastery through the dominance of the mind rather than through physical struggle is made all the more insistent."[11] When Picasso undertook *Boy Leading a Horse*, he was a young, ambitious artist eager to catch the attention of the Parisian art world. According to Varnedoe, the authority Picasso

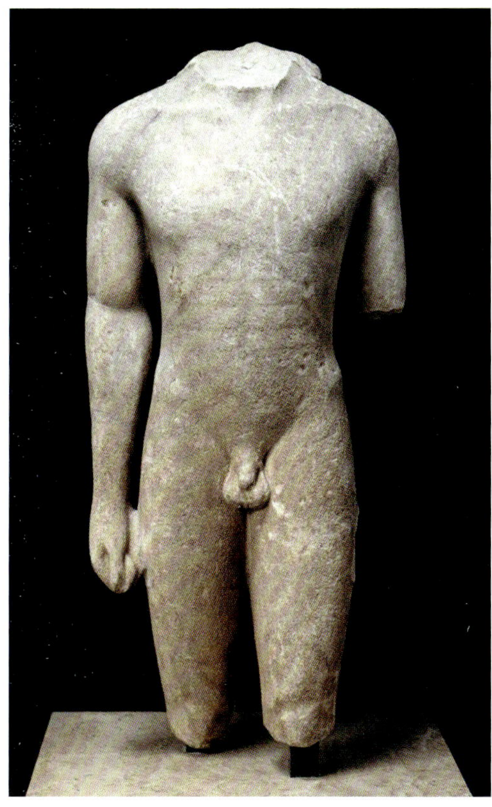

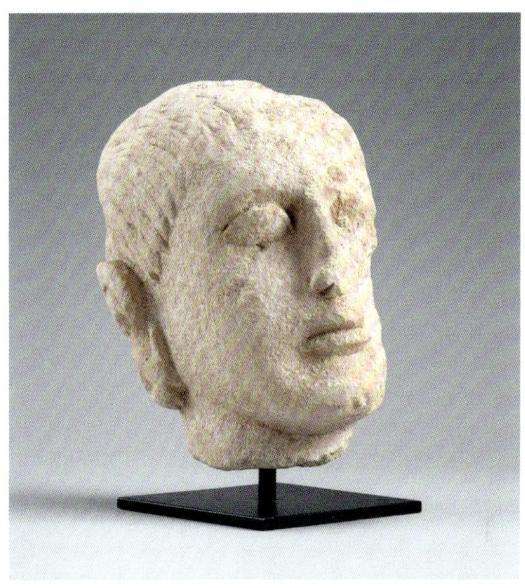

FIG. 9. Kouros. Greek, c. 550 BCE. Marble, 39 ⅜ × 19 ⅛ × 10 ⅝" (100 × 48.5 × 27 cm). MUSÉE DU LOUVRE, PARIS

FIG. 10. Head sculpture. Iberian, found in Cerro de los Santos, Spain, c. 300–200 BCE. Limestone, 8 ⅝ × 4 ⁵⁄₁₆ × 6 ⅞" (22 × 11 × 17.5 cm). MUSÉE DU LOUVRE, PARIS

imparted to the boy appealed to the artist as well: "The scale of the picture, its theme of mastery, the youthful rectitude of the boy—all these announce a new assertiveness and self-confidence in Picasso's approach to his art."[12]

Both qualities—assertiveness and self-confidence—are on full display in the painting. The severe palette of gray and ocher differentiates *Boy Leading a Horse* from Picasso's Blue and early Rose Period works, as well as from those by the Impressionist, Post-Impressionist, and Fauve artists, who overwhelmingly favored brilliant hues and luminous tints. Yet Picasso responded directly to his predecessors and contemporaries in other ways, recasting their innovations in order to make his own art modern. His rendering of the boy, for instance, boldly invokes a variety of artworks produced in different eras, regions, and cultures. The boy's posture resembles that of a type of ancient Greek sculpture known as a kouros, a standing male youth carved from a marble block **[FIG. 9]**. Picasso would have seen kouroi at the Musée du Louvre, where, at the start of 1906, he had also seen an exhibition of ancient Iberian sculptures recently excavated in southern Spain **[FIG. 10]**. These two archaic sources made their mark on *Boy*

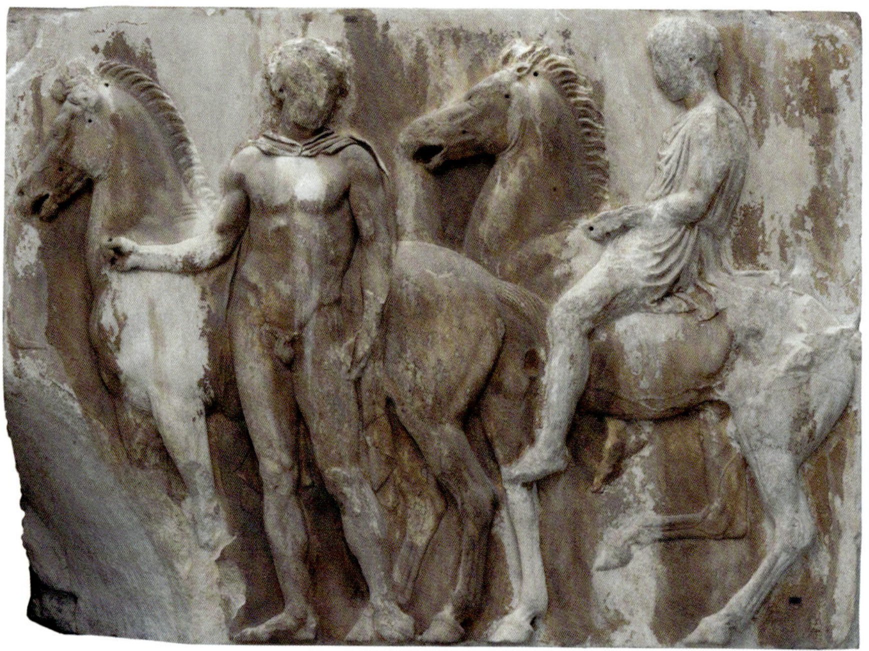

Leading a Horse. The boy's pose—frontal, with one foot in front of the other—evokes kouroi, while his heavy brow, straight nose, full lips, and almond-shaped eyes recall the Iberian heads.

Other sources for *Boy Leading a Horse* may be found through art history, from the Parthenon frieze [**FIG. 11**] to El Greco's *Saint Martin and the Beggar* [**FIG. 12**] and Paul Gauguin's *In the Vanilla Grove, Man and Horse* [**FIG. 13**]. Especially critical was Cézanne's *The Bather* [**FIG. 14**], which Picasso was likely to have been familiar with through Vollard. In 1901 the dealer—whose gallery specialized in avant-garde artists such as Cézanne, Gauguin, Vincent van Gogh, Odilon Redon, and the Nabis—had granted the nineteen-year-old Picasso his first exhibition in Paris.[13] Through his many visits to Galerie Vollard, Picasso came to revere Cézanne, whom he proclaimed his "one and only master."[14] Nonetheless, the origins of *Boy Leading a Horse* have as much to do with Gauguin as with Cézanne.

———

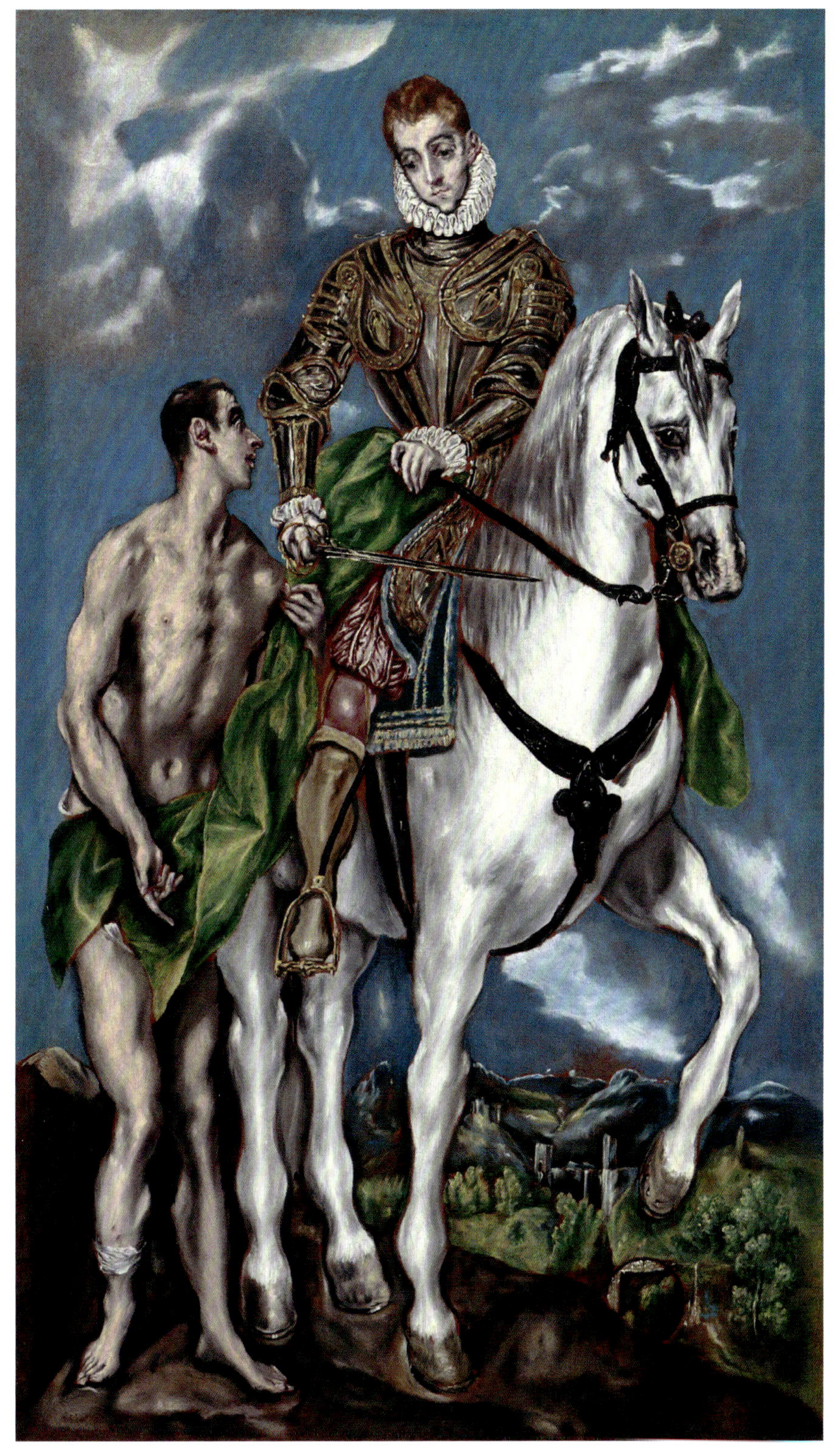

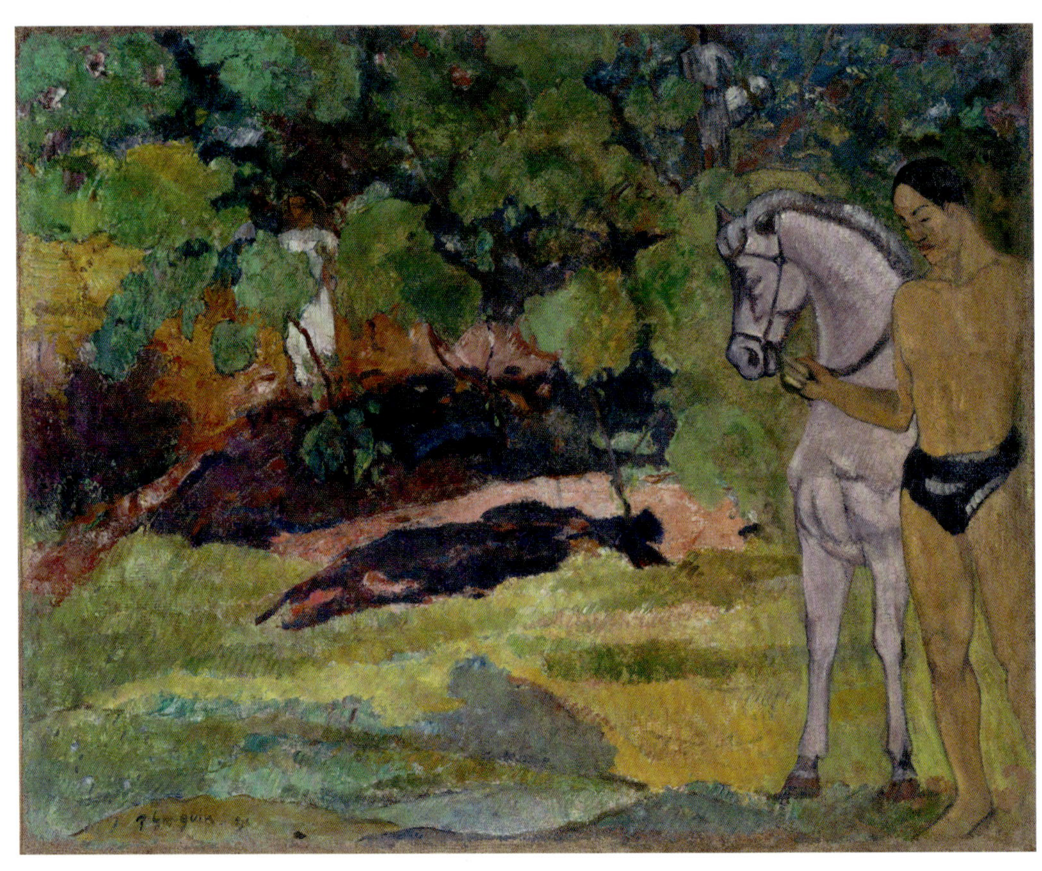

FIG. 13. Paul Gauguin (French, 1848–1903). *In the Vanilla Grove, Man and Horse.* 1891. Oil on canvas, 28 ¾ × 36 ¼" (73 × 92 cm). SOLOMON R. GUGGENHEIM MUSEUM, NEW YORK. THANNHAUSER COLLECTION, GIFT, JUSTIN K. THANNHAUSER

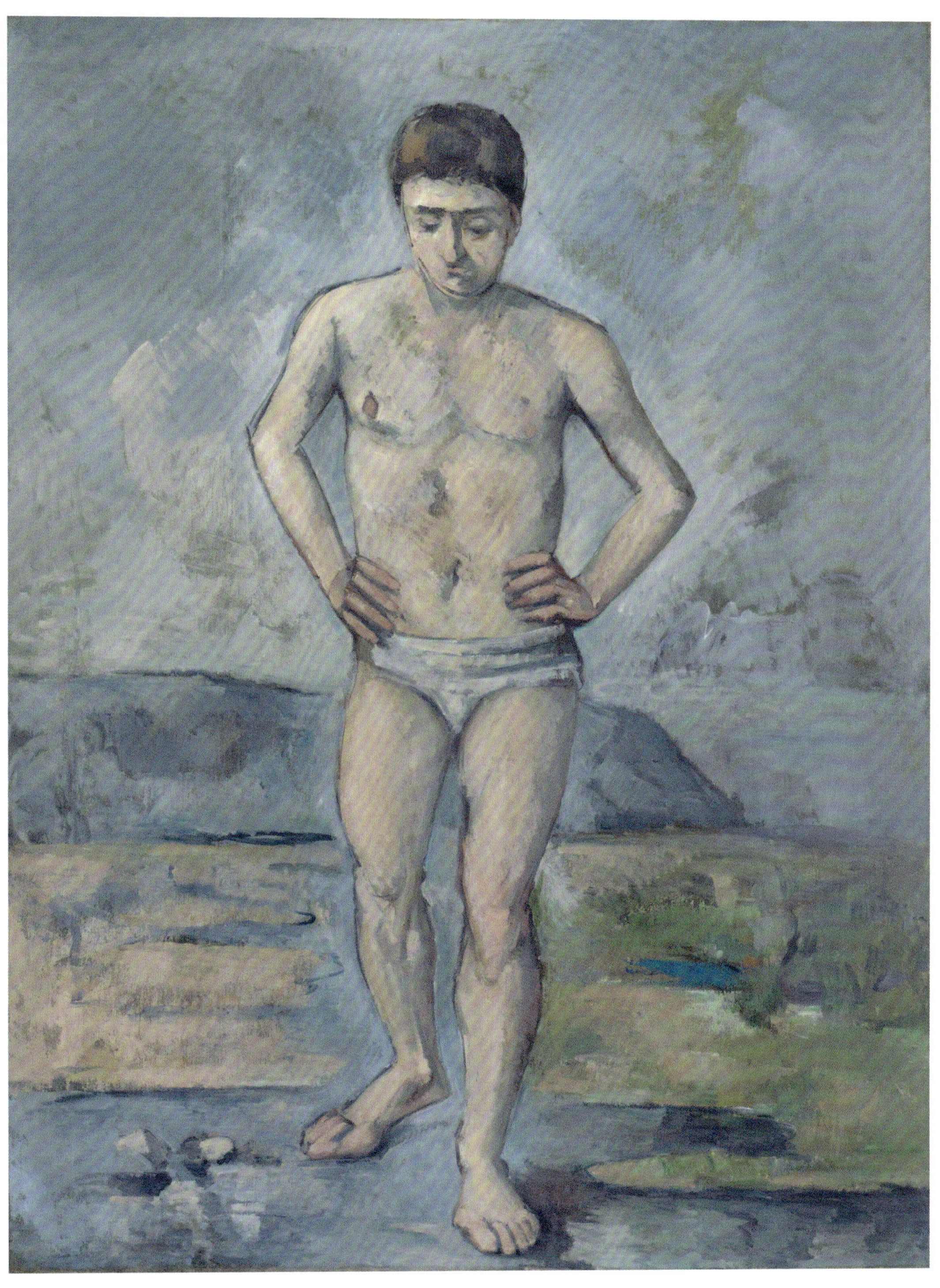

FIG. 14. Paul Cézanne (French, 1839–1906). *The Bather.* c. 1885. Oil on canvas, 50 × 38 ⅛″ (127 × 96.8 cm).
THE MUSEUM OF MODERN ART, NEW YORK. LILLIE P. BLISS COLLECTION

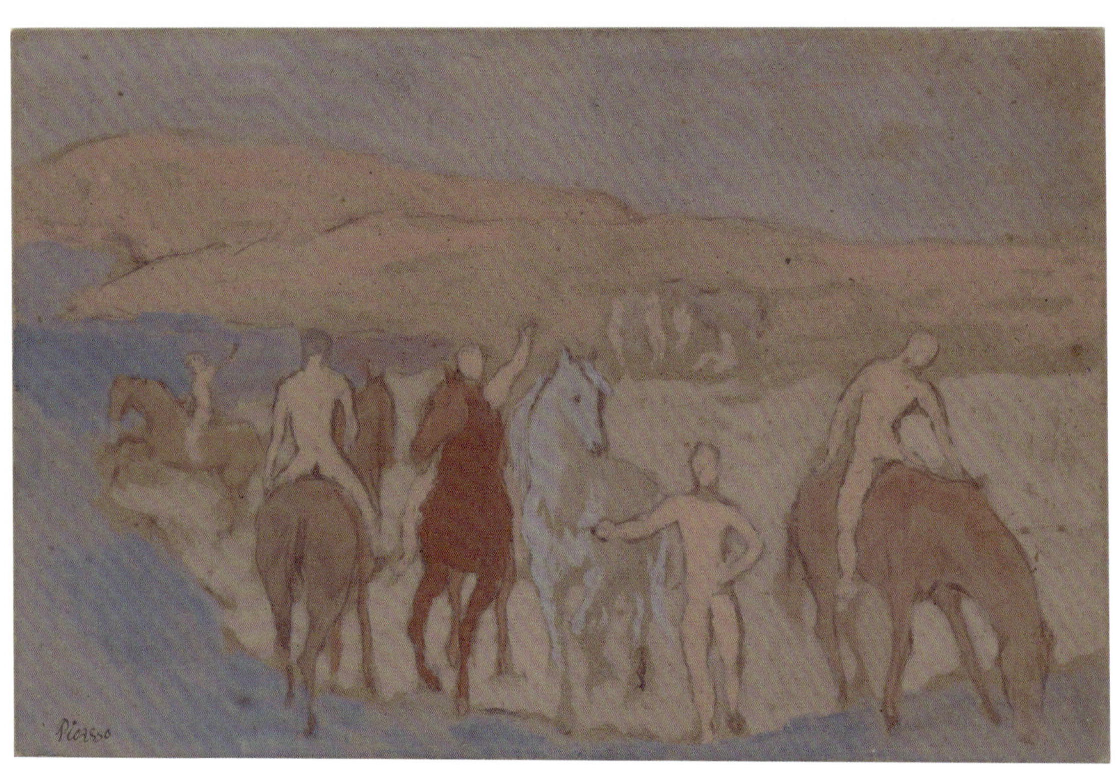

FIG. 15. Pablo Picasso (Spanish, 1881–1973). *The Watering Place*. 1905–06. Gouache on board, 14 ⅞ × 22 ⅞" (37.8 × 58.1 cm). THE METROPOLITAN MUSEUM OF ART, NEW YORK. BEQUEST OF SCOFIELD THAYER

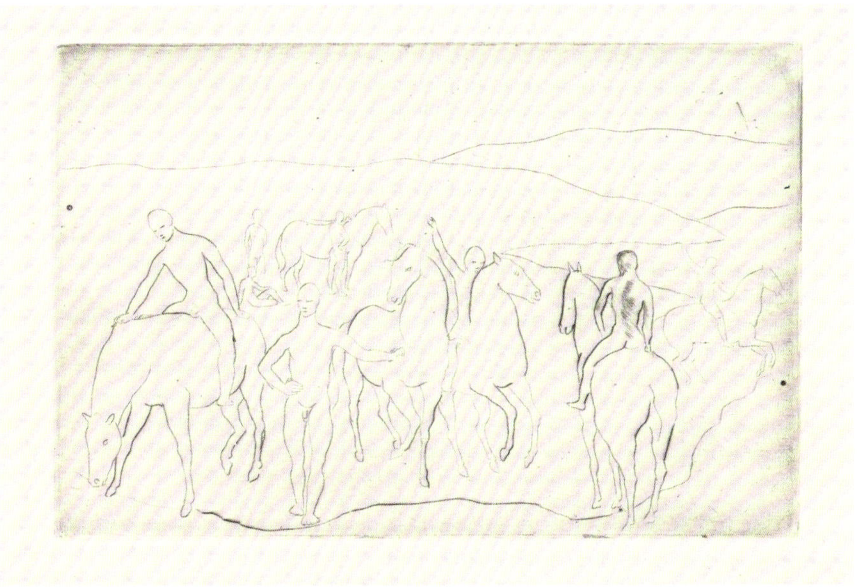

FIG. 16. Pablo Picasso (Spanish, 1881–1973). *The Watering Place (Horses Bathing)* from the Saltimbanques series. 1906, published 1913. Drypoint, plate: 4 ¾ × 7 ⅜" (12.1 × 18.7 cm); sheet: 13 ⅟₁₆ × 19 ¹⁵⁄₁₆" (33.1 × 50.7 cm). Publisher: Ambroise Vollard, Paris. Printer: Louis Fort, Paris. Edition: 250. THE MUSEUM OF MODERN ART, NEW YORK. GIFT OF ABBY ALDRICH ROCKEFELLER

Before *Boy Leading a Horse*, Picasso had executed a number of works depicting boys leading horses. Among them are a gouache sketch **[FIG. 15]** and a drypoint print **[FIG. 16]** with nearly identical compositions: In the foreground, groups of boys accompany their horses to the edge of a broad body of water; in the background, arid hills meet a blank sky. On the basis of these and other comparable works, scholars have proposed that Picasso, in 1905, sought to create an elaborate, large-scale painting of multiple nude boys and bare horses at rest in a barren landscape.

Yet no such painting, it seems, was ever completed. After several months spent working on the project—referred to by scholars as *The Watering Place*—Picasso abandoned it. Or rather, he transformed it into *Boy Leading a Horse*. Because the artist did not date any drawings or paintings associated with either project, precise timelines are elusive. It appears, however, that this transformation played out on paper and canvas throughout the winter of 1905–06, as the central boy-and-horse pair of *The Watering Place* became the sole subject of graphite and watercolor drawings—and, eventually, of *Boy Leading a Horse*. Picasso's working methods during these months were consistent with his broader practice and theory of art: "For me," he later stated, "each painting is a study. I say to myself, I am going one day to finish it, make a finished thing out of it. But as soon as I start to finish it, it becomes another painting."[15] Picasso would prioritize such continuous, iterative study over the course of his decades-long career.

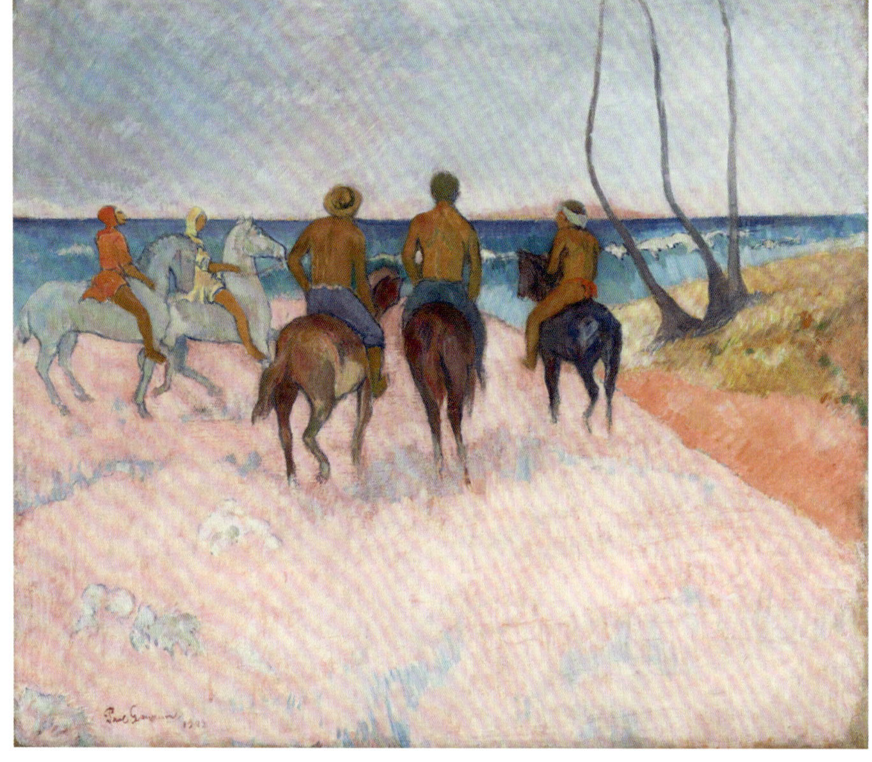

FIG. 17. Paul Gauguin (French, 1848–1903). *Riders on the Beach (I)*. 1902. Oil on canvas, 30 ⅝ × 34 ¹³⁄₁₆″ (77.8 × 88.4 cm). MUSEUM FOLKWANG, ESSEN

He preferred beginnings to endings, questions to answers, process to completion. These preferences—these priorities—are exemplified by the shift from *The Watering Place* to *Boy Leading a Horse*.

The arrangement Picasso was planning for *The Watering Place*—an undeveloped waterfront traversed by several boy-and-horse pairs—closely echoes *Riders on the Beach (I)* and *(II)*, two 1902 paintings by Gauguin that Picasso would have seen at Vollard's gallery [**FIGS. 17, 18**]. Two of Picasso's pairs in the gouache sketch—the one shown from the side (at far left) and the one shown from the rear (at center left)—correspond in posture and orientation to those painted by Gauguin. Picasso idolized the older artist, whose itinerant life and vanguard art served as a model for his own. After studying with the Impressionist painter Camille Pissarro in the 1870s, Gauguin—prompted in part by his travels to so-called primitive locales such as rural France and colonial Tahiti—rejected Realism in favor of Symbolism. His paintings from the 1880s and 1890s conjure deliberately transgressive dreams, memories, and fantasies in strident colors and stylized forms, with settings far removed from the realities of contemporary Paris. Picasso, in *The Watering Place*

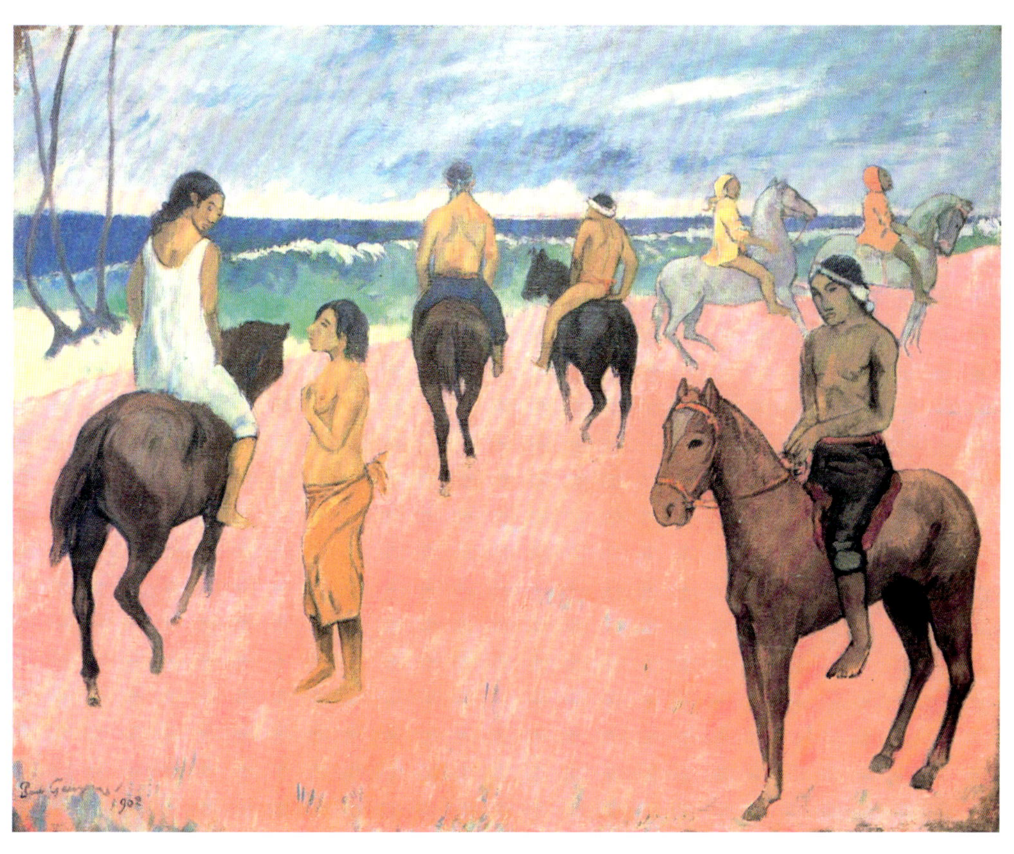

FIG. 18. Paul Gauguin (French, 1848–1903). *Riders on the Beach (II)*. 1902. Oil on canvas, 28 ¾ × 36 ¼" (73 × 92 cm).
PRIVATE COLLECTION

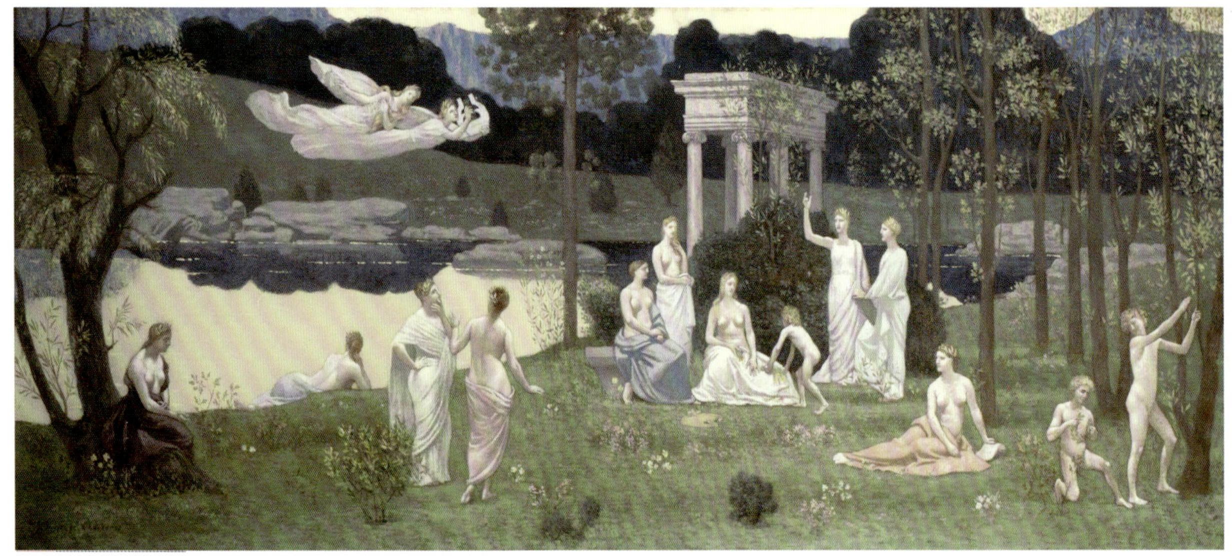

FIG. 19. Pierre Puvis de Chavannes (French, 1824–1898). *The Sacred Grove, Beloved of the Arts and the Muses.* 1884–89. Oil on canvas, 36 ⅝" × 7' 6 ¹⁵⁄₁₆" (93 × 231 cm). THE ART INSTITUTE OF CHICAGO

sketch and print, similarly omitted all signs of the urbanization, industrialization, and commercialization remaking the French capital at the time. Boys and horses roam a terrain without railways, factories, or streetlamps, the boys unconstrained by clothing and the horses unconstrained by tack.

Because of this freedom and the absence of any signs of modernity, scholars have described *The Watering Place* compositions as arcadias—pastoral paradises, untainted by civilization, in which humans and animals live in harmony with nature.[16] In addition to Gauguin's primitivist arcadias, Picasso may have had in mind the classical arcadias of Pierre Puvis de Chavannes, a French artist renowned for his allegorical murals in prominent public buildings [**FIG. 19**]. The faded tonalities and flattened figures in *The Watering Place* sketch, for example, evoke Puvis, as does the drawing's seemingly timeless, placeless setting. Another latter-day arcadia may also have been on Picasso's mind: Matisse's *The Joy of Life* [**FIG. 20**]. According to Rubin, Picasso might have intended his (never realized) *Watering Place* painting as a "competitive riposte" to Matisse, his future friend and rival.[17]

It is unknown what Picasso thought of Matisse or of his art in the winter of 1905–06, when the former was at work on *The Watering Place* and the latter on *The Joy of Life*. Also unknown is why Picasso, at some point during this period, put aside *The Watering Place* and took up *Boy Leading a Horse*. No accounts of his decision survive—no journal entries, no sketchbook annotations, no letters to family or friends. "For reasons we do not know," Rubin speculated,

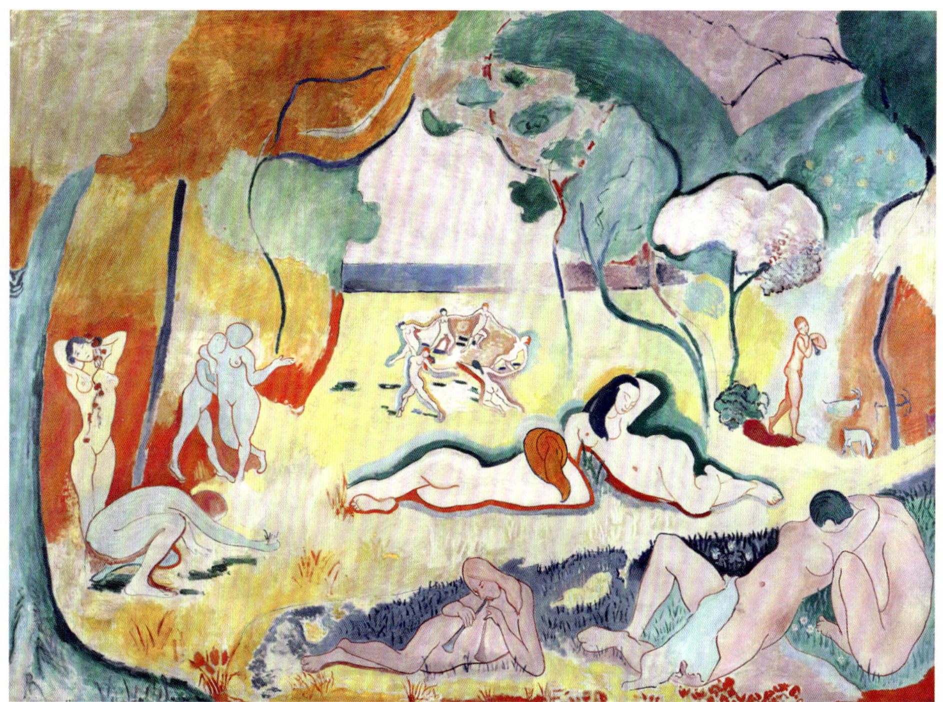

perhaps some dissatisfaction with the composition of *The Watering Place*, perhaps an unwillingness to take on an enormous and time-consuming canvas at a moment when his style had begun rapidly to change— Picasso abandoned his horizontal multifigure project in favor of isolating its central motif in the form of *Boy Leading a Horse*.[18]

Although Picasso's motive for rejecting *The Watering Place* remains ambiguous even today, the rapid stylistic evolution that Rubin mentions was vital to his identity as an artist. "A picture is not thought out and settled beforehand," Picasso asserted in 1935, in one of his few published statements on art. "While it is being done it changes as one's thoughts change."[19] To the artist, it was this capacity for change that marked a break with the art of previous eras: "In the old days pictures went forward toward completion by stages. Every day brought something new. A picture used to be a sum of additions. In my case a picture is a sum of destructions. I do a picture—then I destroy it."[20] Here, Picasso attributes the modernity of his art not to its subject matter but to the contingencies of its making. In the past, he claims, art was the end result of a linear process: artists made plans and then executed them in a sequence of carefully plotted steps.

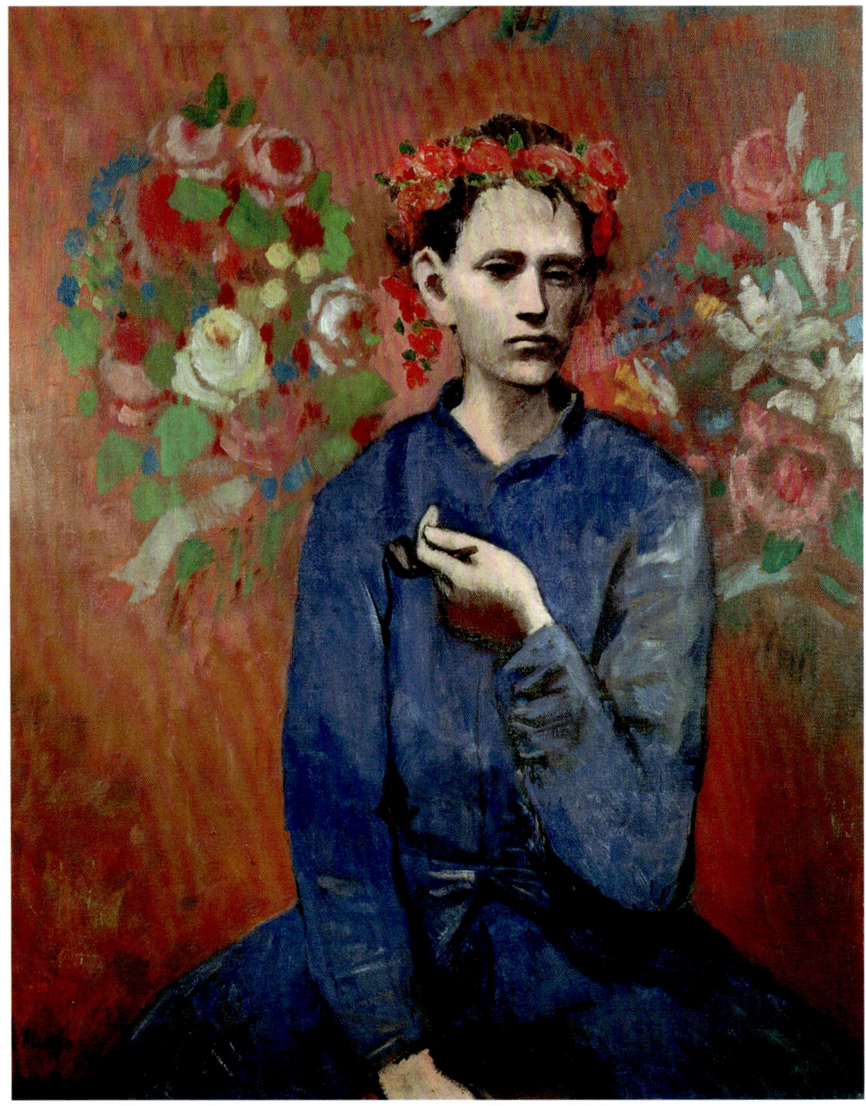

FIG. 21. Pablo Picasso (Spanish, 1881–1973). *Boy with a Pipe*. 1905. Oil on canvas, 39 ⅜ × 32″ (100 × 81.3 cm). PRIVATE COLLECTION

By contrast, he characterizes his own art as the sum total of a dynamic, volatile process with no predetermined procedures or outcomes.

The development of *The Watering Place* and then *Boy Leading a Horse* aligns with this understanding of art making. In 1905, in the Symbolist reverie *Boy with a Pipe* [FIG. 21], Picasso portrayed a Parisian adolescent known as P'tit Louis. Throughout the year, the artist revisited Louis's delicate features in works depicting acrobats, jugglers, and jesters, such as *Two Acrobats with a Dog* [FIG. 22]. Soon these features made their way into drawings associated with *The Watering Place*.

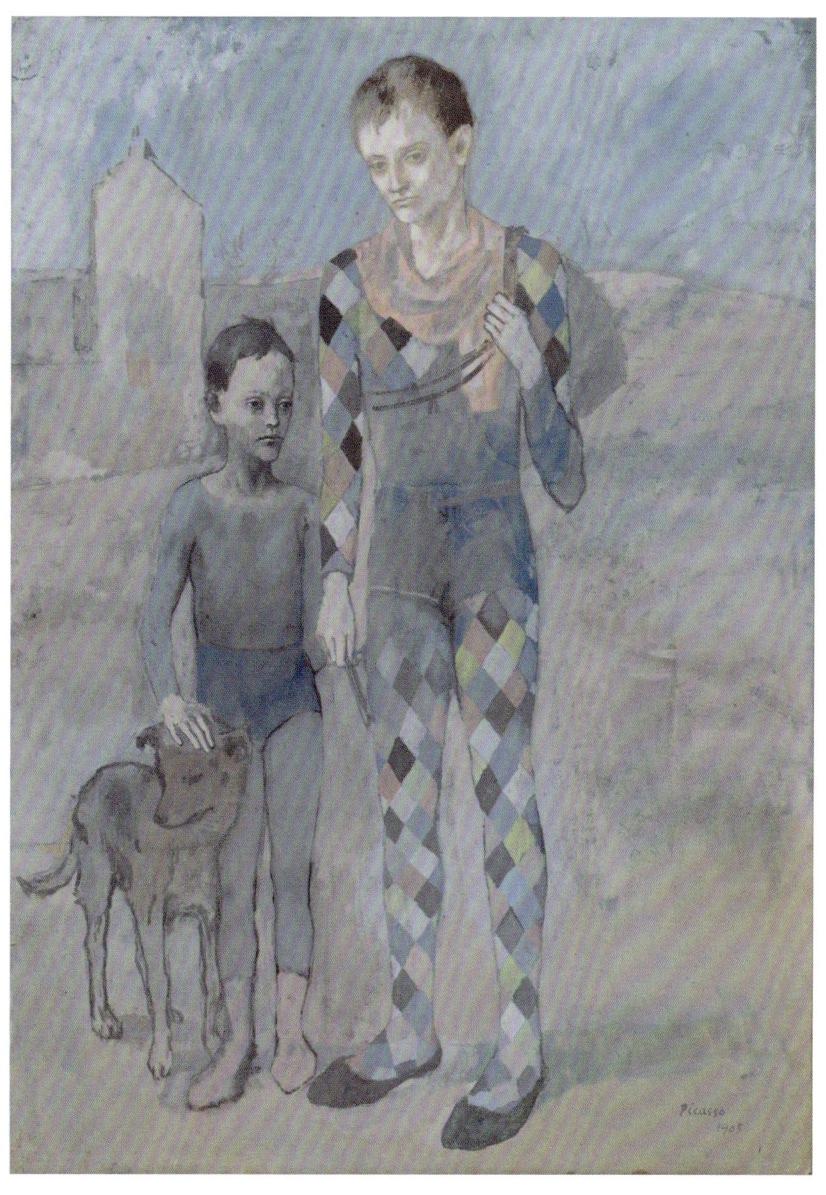

FIG. 22. Pablo Picasso (Spanish, 1881–1973). *Two Acrobats with a Dog.* 1905. Gouache on board, 41 ½ × 29 ½″ (105.5 × 75 cm). THE MUSEUM OF MODERN ART, NEW YORK. GIFT OF MR. AND MRS. WILLIAM A. M. BURDEN

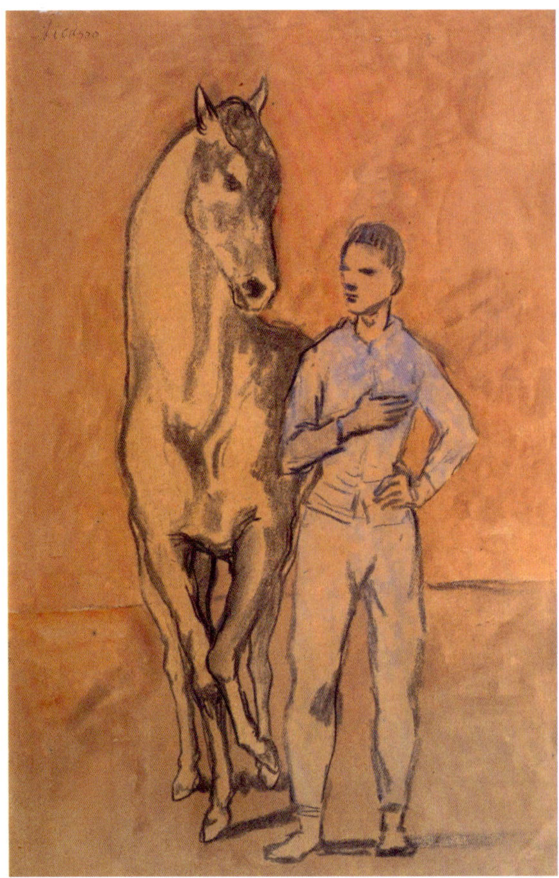

FIG. 23. Pablo Picasso (Spanish, 1881–1973). *Horse with a Youth in Blue.* 1905–06. Watercolor and gouache on paper, 19 ⅝ × 12 ⅝" (49.8 × 32.1 cm). TATE, LONDON. BEQUEATHED BY C. FRANK STOOP

In one of them [FIG. 23], a Louis look-alike standing beside a horse wears the same blue jacket and trousers—typical among French fair and circus performers—seen in *Boy with a Pipe.* But in other drawings [FIGS. 24, 25], the Louis figure has shed his blue costume.

The loss of this costume constituted a pivot. Initially, Picasso seems to have envisioned *The Watering Place* as a companion to *Family of Saltimbanques* [FIG. 26], his largest and most complex Rose Period painting. Similarities in setting, scale, palette, and execution connect the two, as do the boys at their center.[21] Standing in the middle of the earlier painting are two figures who resemble the costumed pair in *Two Acrobats with a Dog.* While devising *The Watering Place,* Picasso maintained an interest in these Louis-like figures but stripped away their costumes—and with their costumes, all references to popular entertainment

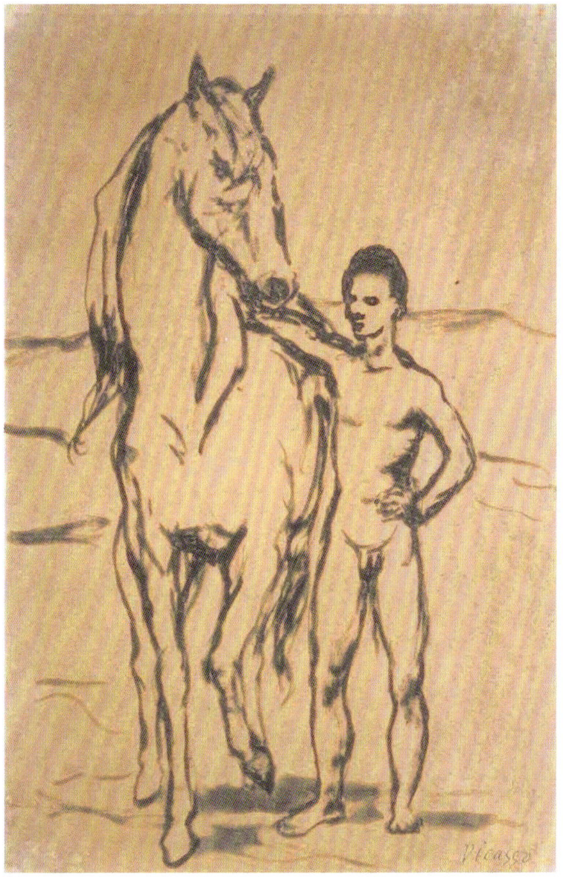

FIG. 24. Pablo Picasso (Spanish, 1881–1973). Study for *Boy Leading a Horse*. 1905–06. Watercolor on paper, 19 ¾ × 12 ¹⁵⁄₁₆" (50.1 × 32.8 cm). BALTIMORE MUSEUM OF ART. THE CONE COLLECTION, FORMED BY DR. CLARIBEL CONE AND MISS ETTA CONE OF BALTIMORE, MARYLAND

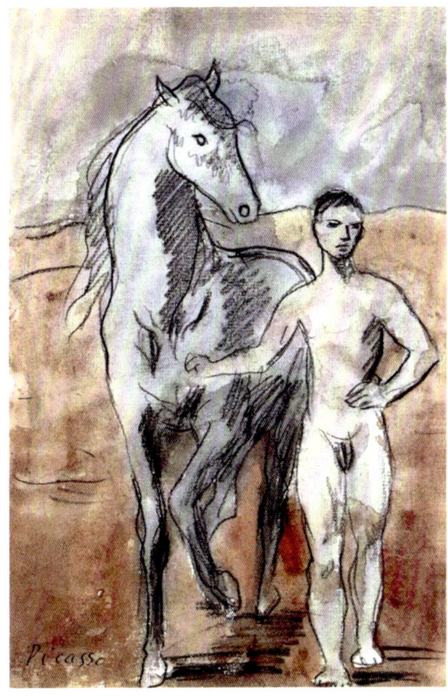

FIG. 25. Pablo Picasso (Spanish, 1881–1973). *Boy Leading a Horse*. 1905–06. Watercolor and conté crayon on paper, 9 ¼ × 6 ³⁄₁₆" (23.5 × 15.7 cm). BALTIMORE MUSEUM OF ART. THE CONE COLLECTION, FORMED BY DR. CLARIBEL CONE AND MISS ETTA CONE OF BALTIMORE, MARYLAND

and contemporary life. "When you begin a picture, you often make some pretty discoveries," the artist cautioned in his 1935 statement. "You must be on guard against these. Destroy the thing, do it over several times."[22]

The creation of *Boy Leading a Horse* accords with this maxim. To start, Picasso conceived a picture: *The Watering Place*. Next, he destroyed this picture: He ditched the composition and dispensed with his many drawings. Yet ultimately these "destructions" proved constructive. By breaking down *The Watering Place*, the artist built up *Boy Leading a Horse*. This, too, agreed with his conception of the creative process. "In the end," he clarified in the 1935 statement, "nothing is lost: the red I took away from one place turns up somewhere else."[23] For Picasso, perpetual transformation was a means to an end, and an end in itself. His preoccupation with

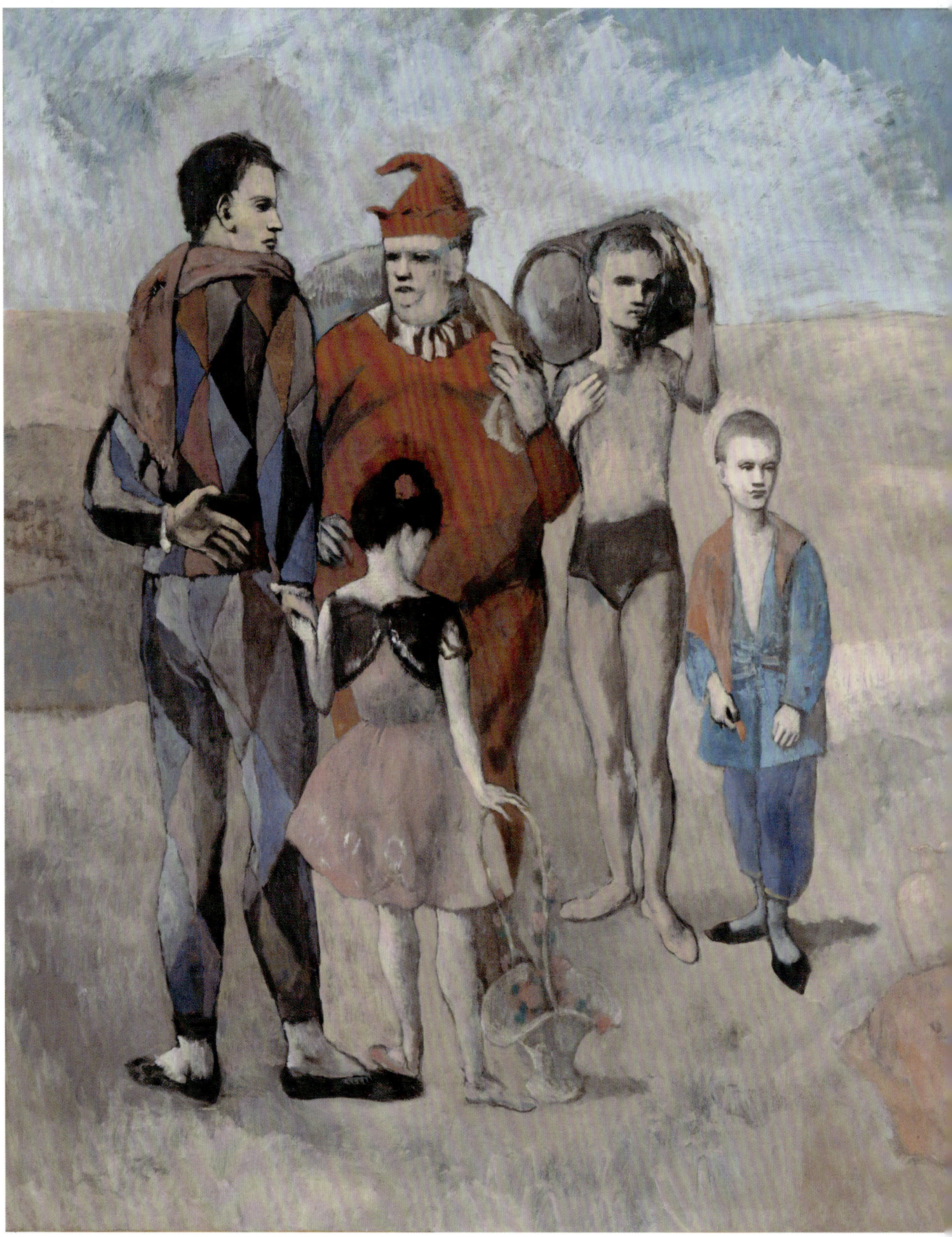

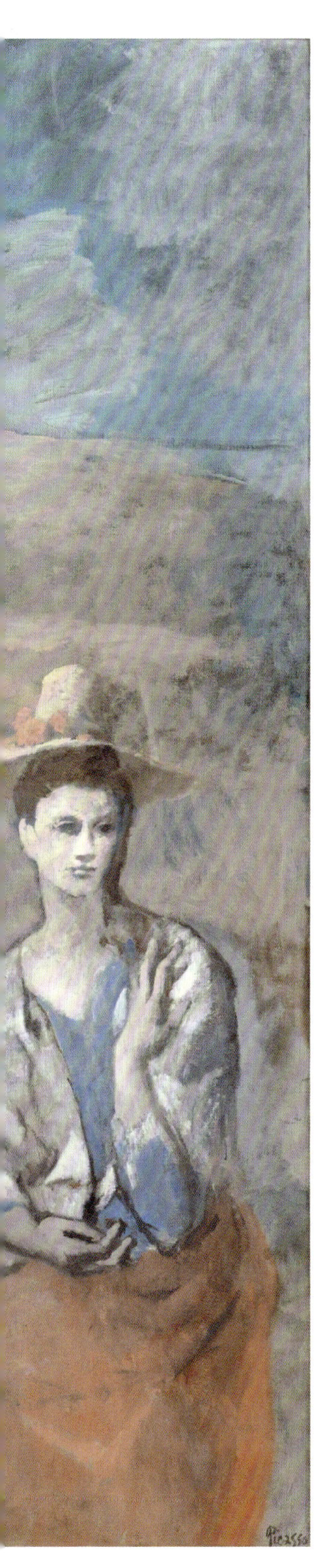

FIG. 26. Pablo Picasso (Spanish, 1881–1973). *Family of Saltimbanques.* 1905. Oil on canvas, 6′ 11 ¾″ × 7′ 6 ⅜″ (212.8 × 229.6 cm). NATIONAL GALLERY OF ART, WASHINGTON, DC. CHESTER DALE COLLECTION

change—both personal and creative—can be traced to the frequent relocations and persistent artistic experiments of his early years.

———

By the time Picasso embarked on *Boy Leading a Horse,* he had long considered himself an artistic prodigy, as had his family and friends. Born in 1881 in Málaga, a coastal city in southern Spain, Pablo Ruiz Picasso was raised by parents—and supported by relatives—who believed deeply in his talent. "When I was a child," he recalled, "my mother said to me, 'If you become a soldier you'll be a general. If you become a monk you'll end up as the Pope.' Instead, I became a painter and wound up as Picasso."[24]

As a child, Picasso was encouraged to draw by his father, an academic artist and art teacher. The young artist's first signed, dated drawing depicts Hercules— the Roman hero famous for his strength—wielding a club with a raised arm and with his legs bent and torso twisted [**FIG. 27**]. Picasso made this drawing when he was nine years old, yet he later dismissed the idea that it, or any works from his youth, resembled drawings by others his age: "I never did children's drawings. Never."[25] Throughout his career, Picasso would cite his boyhood draftsmanship as evidence of his innate technical and imaginative capabilities.

If precocity was one element of Picasso's self-conception as an artist, another was conflict. In 1891 he moved with his family from Málaga to the port city of A Coruña, in Galicia, in northwestern Spain. There he enrolled in a local art academy, where his father had obtained a teaching position. By his own account, he was a gifted but difficult student: "I remember at the School of Fine Arts they made us write in a notebook— 'One must learn to paint.' I did it, but in reverse. I wrote, 'One must not learn to paint. One must not learn to paint. One must not learn to paint.'"[26] Throughout his life, Picasso associated art making with defiance. In his view, a true artist resisted rules, formulas, and conventions, both in and out of the studio.

In Barcelona, the Mediterranean metropolis where his family established a permanent home in 1895, Picasso's contrarian spirit surged. Once again his father had accepted a teaching position at the local art academy. And once again Picasso registered for classes there, then clashed with his teachers. With friends from the academy, he expanded his cultural education outside the classroom, exploring the city's cosmopolitan cafes and theaters [**FIG. 28**]. As he gained exposure to avant-garde artistic movements such as Symbolism, he began to bristle at his academic training and envision alternatives to it. His father, how- ever, had other plans for him.

As an unsuccessful artist who had turned to teaching to support his family, José Ruiz wanted his son to specialize in religious painting—a practical choice for making a living in predominantly Catholic Spain. Under the close supervision

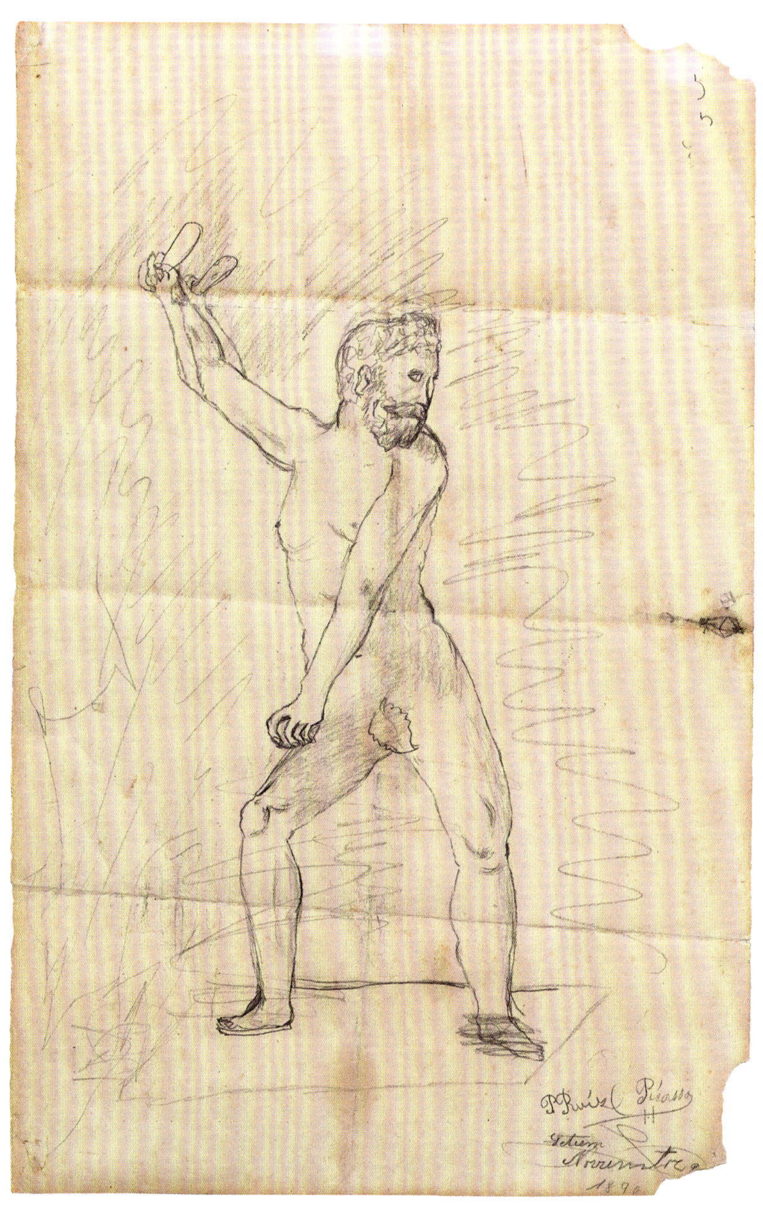

FIG. 27. Pablo Picasso (Spanish, 1881–1973). *Hercules.* 1890. Pencil on paper, 19 ½ × 12 ⅝″ (49.6 × 32 cm). MUSEU PICASSO, BARCELONA. GIFT OF THE ARTIST

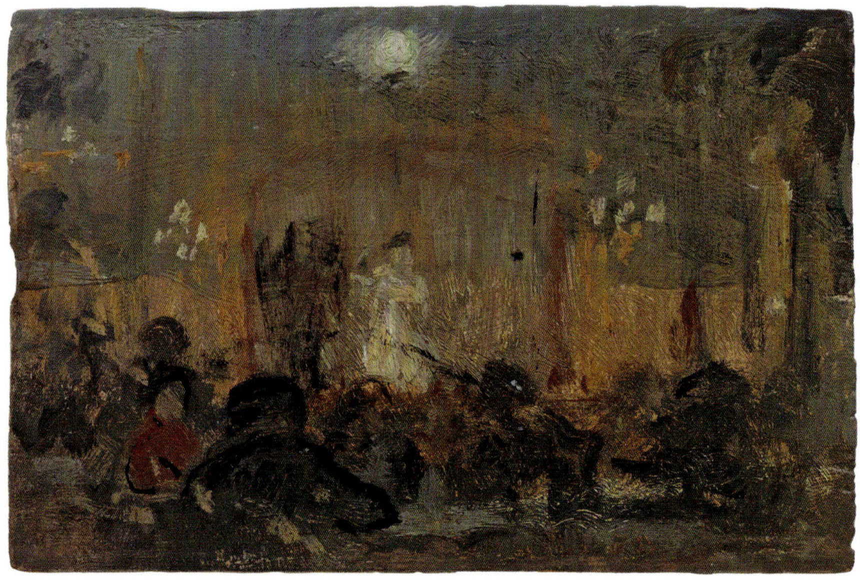

of his father, Picasso completed several well-received religious paintings while still in his teens. Spurred by the success of one, *Science and Charity* [FIG. 29], which won an honorable mention at Spain's Exposición General de Bellas Artes in 1897, the young artist left for Madrid in order to study at the prestigious Real Academia de Bellas Artes de San Fernando. Yet he disliked the city, and he loathed his teachers. "They have no common sense," he complained in a letter to a friend. "If I had a son who wanted to be a painter, I wouldn't keep him in Spain for a moment."[27] In 1899 Picasso returned to Barcelona, determined to set his own personal and professional course.

Self Portrait (Yo), from 1901, attests to this newfound independence [FIG. 30]. The artist stares directly at the viewer, his face and body described with slashing strokes of reds, blues, and greens. Brash self-confidence has replaced the piety of *Science and Charity*; vivid colors and jagged brushstrokes replaced the earlier painting's restrained palette and tidy execution. Notably, the signature at the lower right of the self-portrait reads "Picasso": It was around this time that the artist began using his mother's surname instead of, as was typical in Spain, his father's. "[Picasso is] more unique, more musical than Ruiz," he later explained. "Can you imagine me being called Ruiz? Pablo Ruiz?"[28] His adopted surname, he added, linked him to artists he admired: "Have you ever noticed that there's a double *s* in Matisse, in Poussin, in Rousseau?"[29]

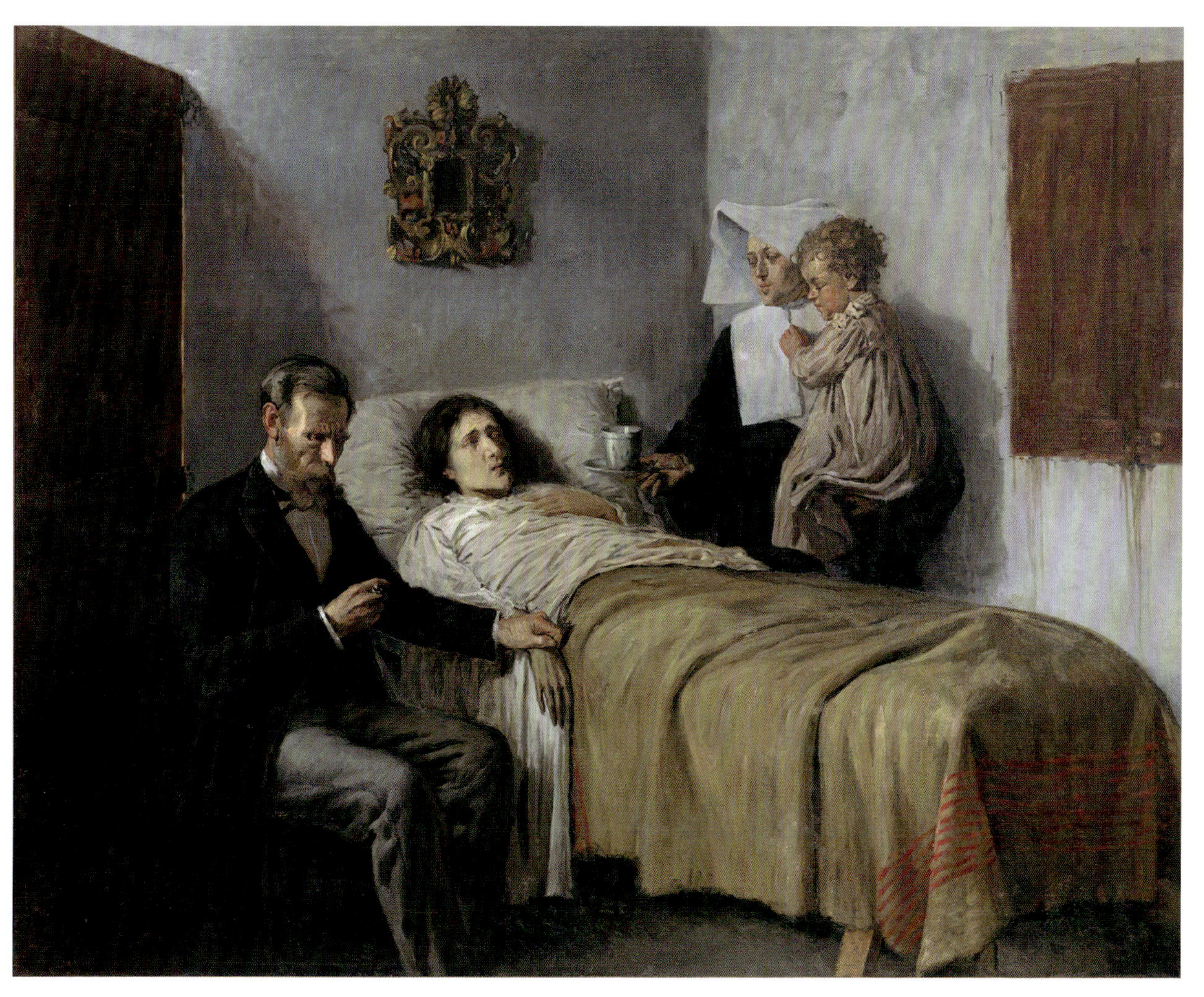

FIG. 29. Pablo Picasso (Spanish, 1881–1973). *Science and Charity*. 1897. Oil on canvas, 6′ 5 ¾″ × 8′ 2 ⁷⁄₁₆″ (197.5 × 250 cm). MUSEU PICASSO, BARCELONA. GIFT OF THE ARTIST

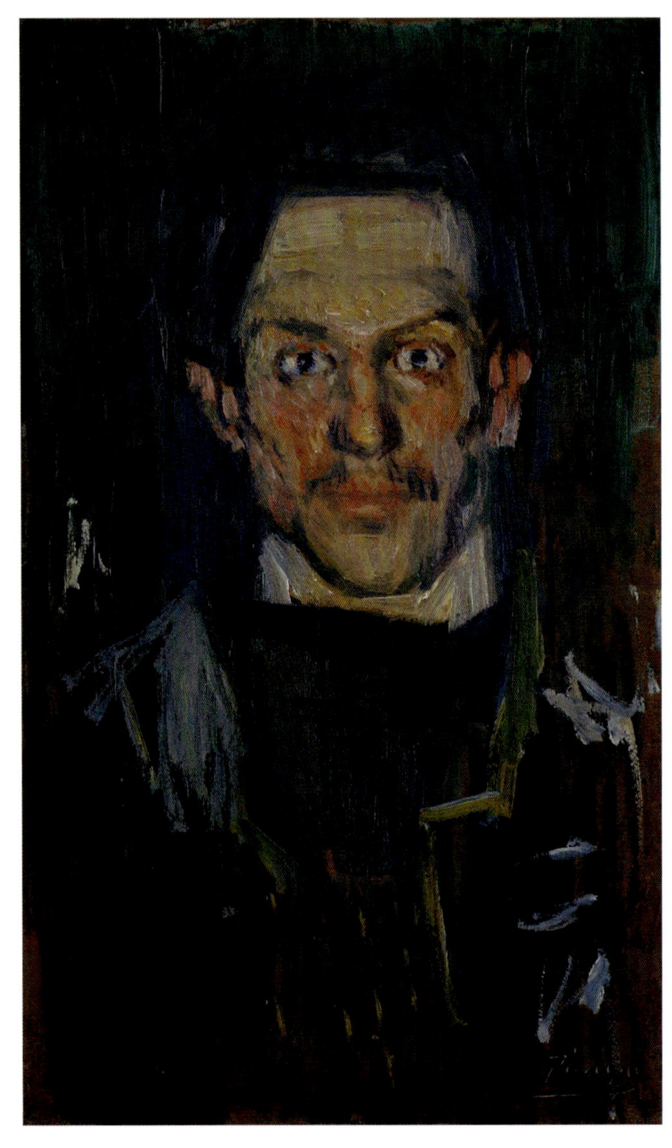

FIG. 30. Pablo Picasso (Spanish, 1881–1973). *Self Portrait (Yo)*. 1901. Oil on cardboard mounted on wood, 20 ¼ × 12 ½″ (51.4 × 31.8 cm). THE MUSEUM OF MODERN ART, NEW YORK. MRS. JOHN HAY WHITNEY BEQUEST

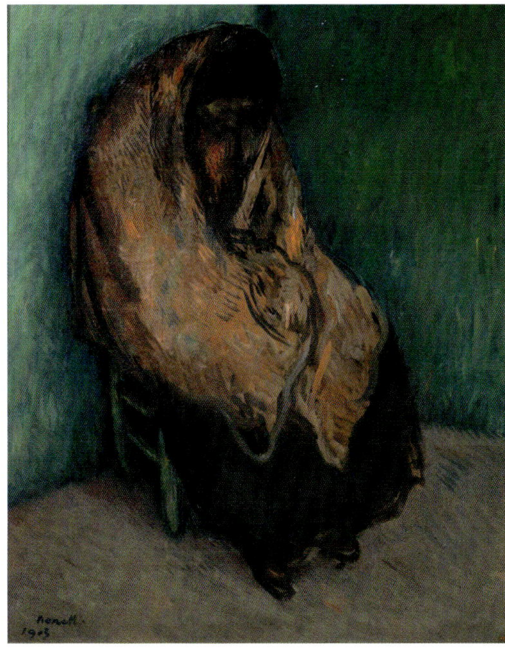

FIG. 31. Isidre Nonell (Spanish, 1872–1911). *Dolores.* 1902–03. Oil on canvas, 64 × 51 9/16" (162.5 × 131 cm). MUSEU NACIONAL D'ART DE CATALUNYA, BARCELONA. PLANDIURA COLLECTION, PURCHASE

The overt change in style from *Science and Charity* to *Self Portrait (Yo)* charts Picasso's break with the academic teachings of his father and his deepening involvement with Catalan *modernisme*. Galvanized by modernist movements all over Europe, the *modernistes* aimed to advance art, literature, music, architecture, and design in Catalonia, an urbanized, industrialized region in northeastern Spain.[30] Established members of the movement such as Ramon Casas, Joan Maragall, and Santiago Rusiñol introduced fresh European cultural tendencies to Barcelona, the region's capital. Meanwhile, younger *modernistes* such as Ricard Canals, Joaquim Mir, Isidre Nonell, and Ramon Pichot were immersing themselves in Barcelona's outlying neighborhoods, portraying run-down streets and destitute residents—subjects not typically considered suitable for art—with a formal vocabulary shaped by Impressionism and Post-Impressionism **[FIG. 31]**.[31]

In keeping with his Catalan peers, Picasso focused on scenes of poverty and despair in the years around 1900. In a print from 1904, a haggard couple finishes a meager meal of wine and bread **[FIG. 32]**; in a watercolor from the same year, a hunched woman, awash in blue, leans on her frail arms **[FIG. 33]**. These melancholy compositions were informed by the artist's experiences of hardship in that period. Devastated by the death of a close friend and struggling to support himself through his art, Picasso traveled frequently between Spain and France in an effort to further his career, all the while depicting angular figures in somber

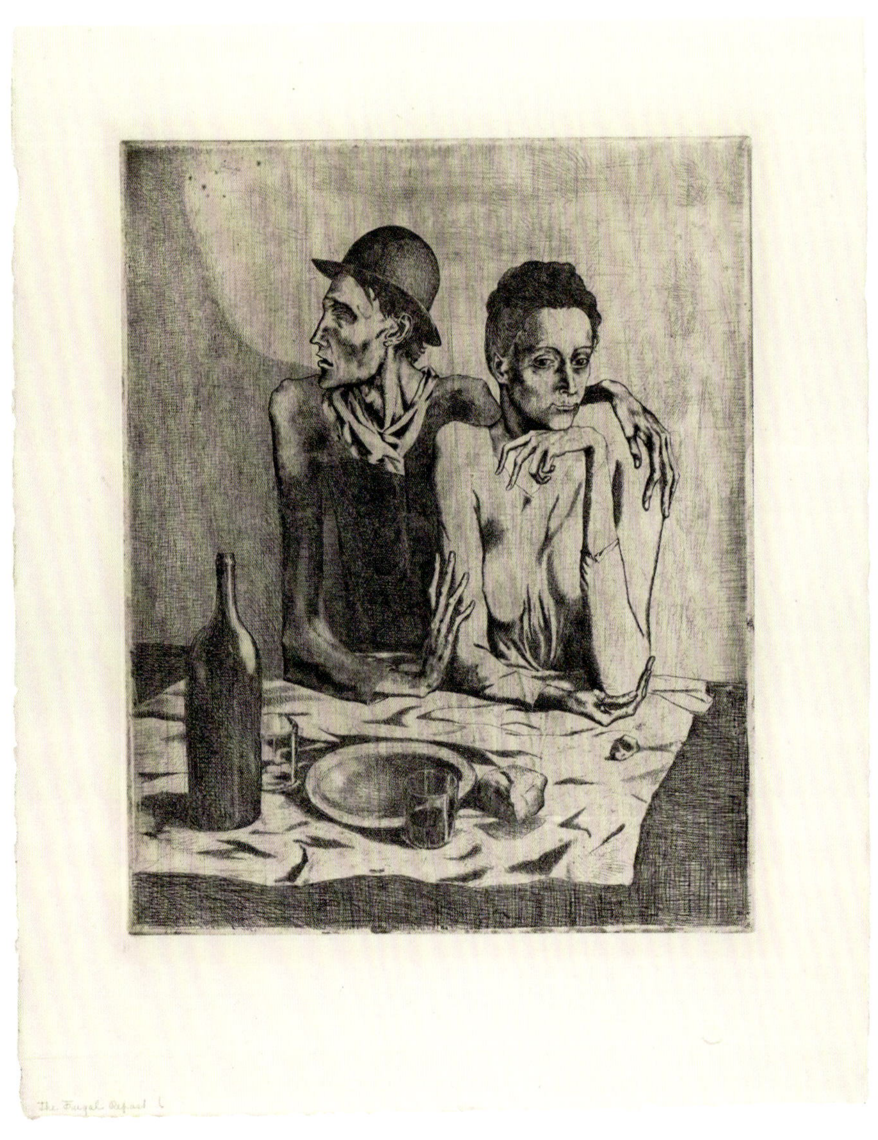

FIG. 32. Pablo Picasso (Spanish, 1881–1973). *The Frugal Repast* from the Saltimbanques series. 1904, published 1913. Etching, plate: 18 ¼ × 14 ¹³⁄₁₆″ (46.3 × 37.7 cm). Publisher: Ambroise Vollard, Paris. Printer: Louis Fort, Paris. Edition: 250. THE MUSEUM OF MODERN ART, NEW YORK. GIFT OF ABBY ALDRICH ROCKEFELLER

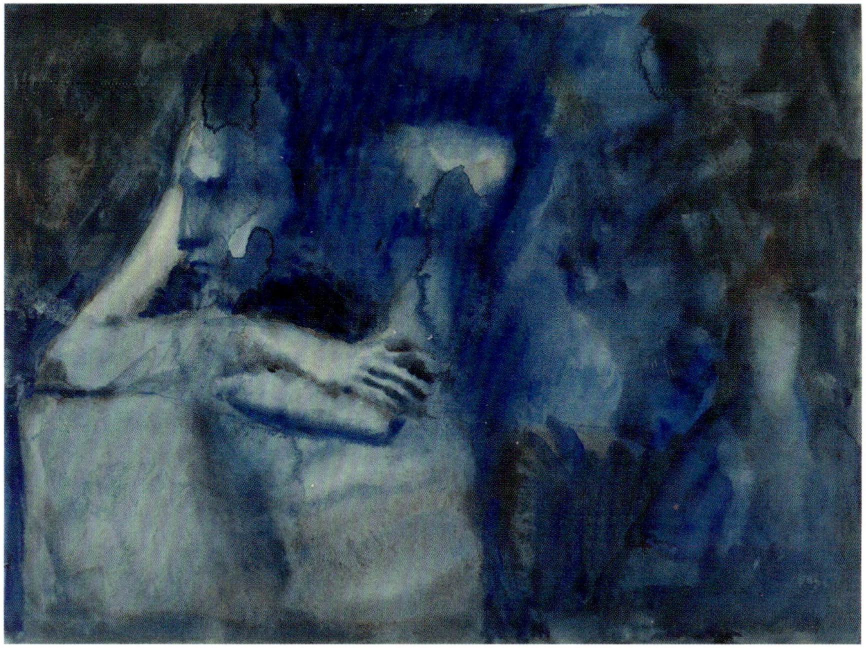

FIG. 33. Pablo Picasso (Spanish, 1881–1973). *Brooding Woman* (recto). 1904. Watercolor on paper, 10 ⅝ × 14 ½" (27 × 36.8 cm). THE MUSEUM OF MODERN ART, NEW YORK. GIFT OF MR. AND MRS. WERNER E. JOSTEN

hues and with gaping shadows in paintings, drawings, and prints. These were the years of his Blue Period.

But blue, in mid-1904, gave way to dusty reds, pinks, and creams. The start of Picasso's Rose Period coincided with his permanent move to Paris, where a string of exhibitions led to his first critical and financial successes. As important as the artist's lightening palette and themes—most notably, performers modeled on those he observed at Parisian cabarets and circuses—were his burgeoning relationships with like-minded artists, writers, and musicians. He settled in a studio in Montmartre, in a dilapidated building known as the Bateau-Lavoir (Laundry boat) on account of its narrow hallways, creaking floorboards, and rudimentary plumbing. Over the years, his neighbors included the painters Canals, André Derain, Juan Gris, Amedeo Modigliani, and Maurice de Vlaminck. His closest friends, though, were poets: Guillaume Apollinaire, Max Jacob, and André Salmon, whose likenesses can be detected in Picasso's *Family of Saltimbanques*.[32]

The Bateau-Lavoir, for the so-called *bande à Picasso* (Picasso gang), was a place of close bonds, late nights, and creative ferment. When Kees van Dongen, a fellow resident, later pictured the building in an illustration for a 1949 memoir by the writer and Montmartre dweller Roland Dorgelès, he opted for an instantly recognizable scene: Picasso in his Bateau-Lavoir studio, wearing blue

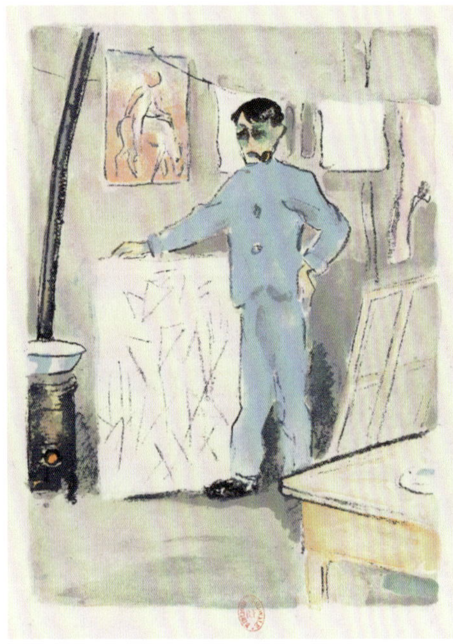

FIG. 34. Kees van Dongen (Dutch, 1877–1968). *Picasso in His Studio,* in Roland Dorgelès, *Au beau temps de la butte* (Paris: Nouvelle Librairie de France, 1949)

coveralls—his work uniform at the time—and standing beside a stove, canvas, and clothesline [**FIG. 34**]. The sole identifiable artwork in the image—hanging on the wall behind him—is *Nude Boy on a Horse,* which he painted in 1906 in tandem with *Boy Leading a Horse* and gave to van Dongen that same year.[33] The appearance of the former painting in van Dongen's illustration, made decades later, suggests a close association of Picasso with his *Watering Place* offshoots during a time of stylistic evolution; viewed together, *Boy Leading a Horse* and *Nude Boy on a Horse* are a testament to the strength of the upheaval.

———

Over the same winter in which he painted *Boy Leading a Horse,* Picasso undertook a portrait of Gertrude Stein. Stein commissioned the portrait in 1905 and posed for Picasso in his studio through the first half of 1906. But the artist, she later wrote, grew frustrated with her likeness after eighty or ninety sittings (probably an exaggeration on Stein's part): "All of a sudden one day Picasso painted out the whole head," she recounted. "I can't see you any longer when I look, he said irritably."[34]

Picasso paused the portrait in May 1906, when he left Paris for Gósol, a Catalan village in the Pyrenees, where he spent the summer. During his time there, he drew and painted many nude youths that recall the figure in *Boy Leading a Horse* [**FIG. 35**]. His Gósol boys have similarly pared-down physiques,

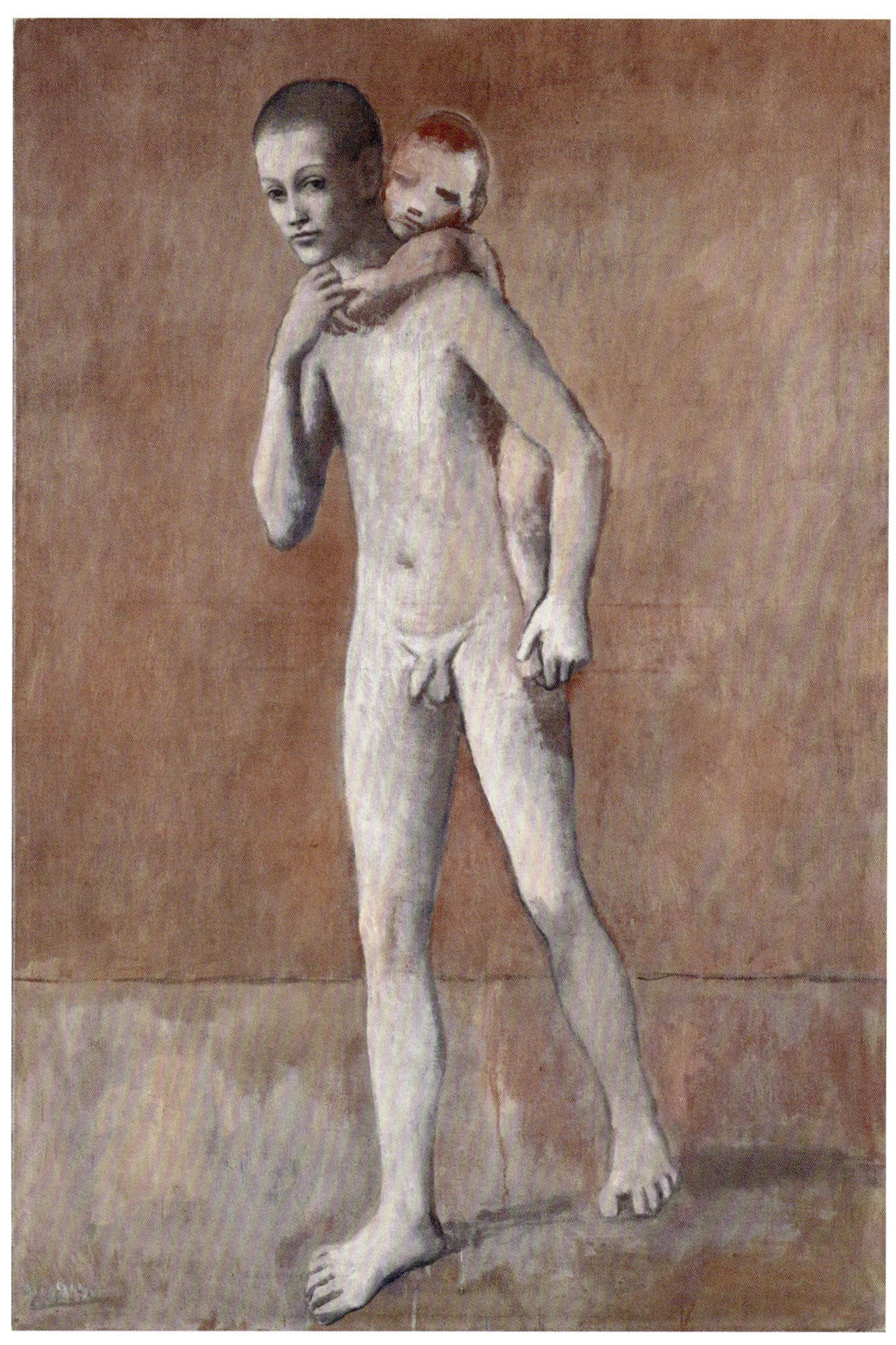

FIG. 35. Pablo Picasso (Spanish, 1881–1973). *The Two Brothers*. Early summer 1906. Oil on canvas, 55 $^{11}/_{16}$ × 38 ¼″ (141.4 × 97.1 cm). KUNSTMUSEUM BASEL

sculpted faces, and mysterious affects; moreover, they occupy similarly timeless, placeless environments. Upon returning to Paris, Picasso applied these qualities to *Gertrude Stein*, simplifying Stein's body and backdrop and portraying her face as a high-relief mask [**FIG. 36**]. Yet her chiseled eyes, nose, mouth, and chin are represented from slightly different vantages, and the distance between background and foreground is collapsed. The final portrait thus hints at the fractured forms, composite perspectives, and constricted space distinctive to Cubism, the revolutionary style that Picasso and Georges Braque would invent in 1907.

While Gertrude Stein was pleased with her portrait, Leo Stein deemed it "incoherent."[35] He complained, in pejorative language, that Picasso had relied on African art—inferior to European art, he implied—to resolve it. Leo also disapproved of *Les Demoiselles d'Avignon*—a "horrible mess"—and he denounced Cubism as unintelligible.[36] For him, one suspects, the problem was change itself, exemplified by the startling shift Picasso had made, between 1906 and 1907, from the austere classicism of *Boy Leading a Horse* to the explosive proto-Cubism of *Les Demoiselles d'Avignon*. "If it was not one thing," Leo wrote of Picasso's many enthusiasms, "it was another."[37] Gertrude, however, reveled in the speed and thoroughness of what the artist himself called his "metamorphoses."[38] "We were young then," she wrote of herself and Picasso in *The Autobiography of Alice B. Toklas*, her 1933 modernist memoir. "We did a great deal in a year."[39]

In 1914 Gertrude and Leo Stein parted ways over their growing aesthetic differences.[40] They sold much of their collection, and *Boy Leading a Horse* ended up first in Berlin, in the collection of the German-Jewish banker Paul von Mendelssohn-Bartholdy; then in Munich, in the collection of the German-Jewish art dealer and Picasso specialist Justin Thannhauser; and finally in Lucerne, in the collection of Thannhauser's cousin and business partner, Siegfried Rosengart. Created by an artist whom the Nazis distrusted and owned by collectors whom they persecuted, *Boy Leading a Horse* faced an uncertain future in the years prior to World War II, as the Nazis and their collaborators routinely seized artworks from public and private collections, destroying some and selling others.[41] But in 1936 the American media executive William Paley acquired *Boy Leading a Horse* in Switzerland and transported it to his home in New York. A noted collector and longtime trustee of The Museum of Modern Art, Paley regularly lent *Boy Leading a Horse* to the institution before donating it in 1964.

At the Museum the painting has starred in landmark exhibitions, from *Art in Our Time* (1939) to *Pablo Picasso: A Retrospective* (1980). As a hinge between the artist's pre- and post-1906 works, *Boy Leading a Horse* illuminates the meaning of modern art to Picasso and the meaning of Picasso to modern art. Its presence in MoMA's collection fulfills Barr's wish that these two important stories be told together.

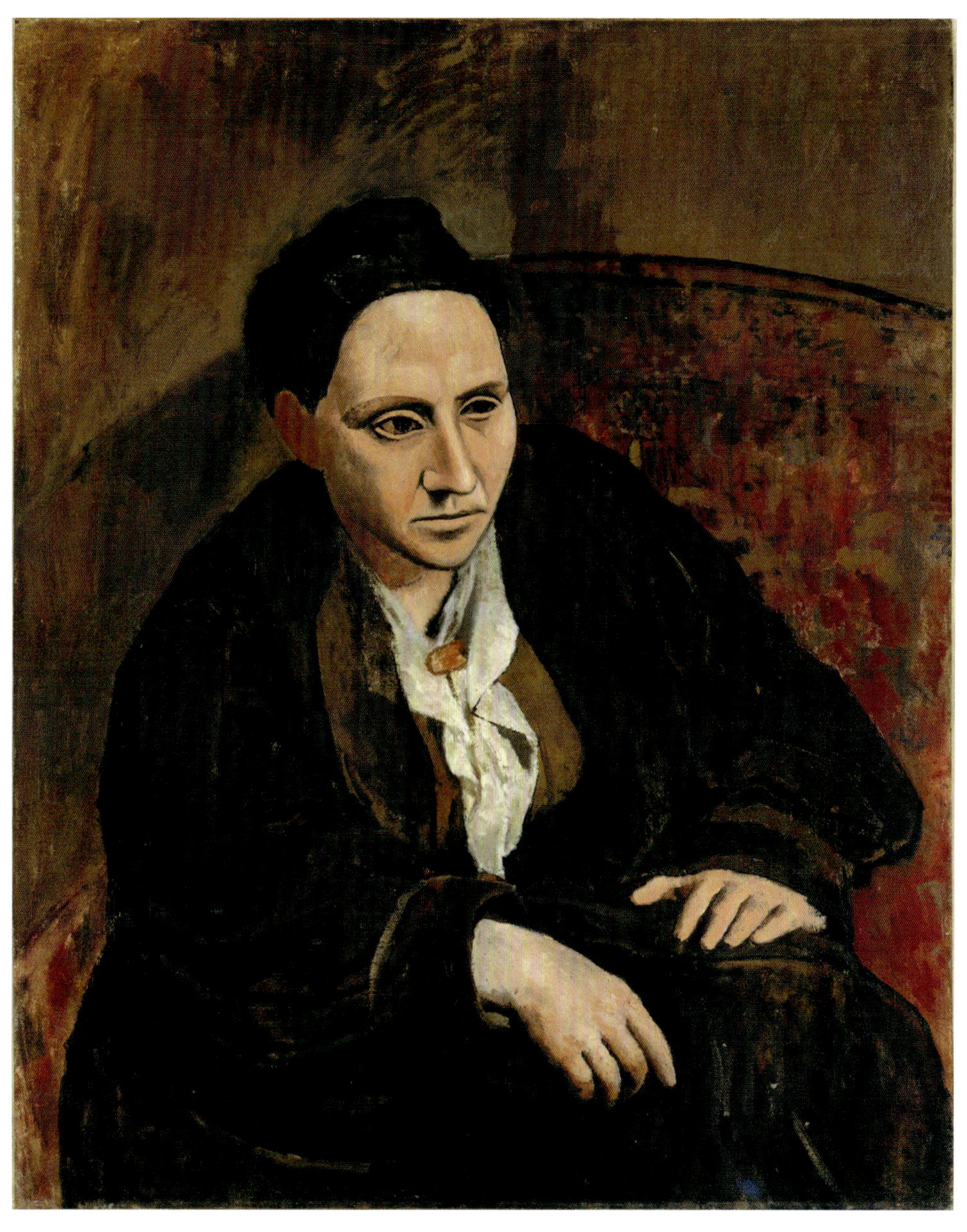

FIG. 36. Pablo Picasso (Spanish, 1881–1973). *Gertrude Stein*. 1905–06. Oil on canvas, 39 ⅜ × 32″ (100 × 81.3 cm).
THE METROPOLITAN MUSEUM OF ART, NEW YORK. BEQUEST OF GERTRUDE STEIN

NOTES

1. Alfred H. Barr Jr., *Picasso: Fifty Years of His Art* (New York: The Museum of Modern Art, 1946), 9.

2. Barr, *Picasso*, 9.

3. Gustave Coquiot, *Cubistes, futuristes, passéistes*, 1914, excerpt trans. by Christine Baker and published in Robert J. Boardingham, "Critical Origins of Picasso's 'Blue' and 'Rose' Periods," in in Marilyn McCully, ed., *Picasso: The Early Years, 1892–1906* (Washington, DC: National Gallery of Art, 1997), 147.

4. Barr, *Picasso*, 42.

5. Leo Stein, *Appreciation: Painting, Poetry and Prose* (1947; rev. ed. Lincoln: University of Nebraska Press, 1996), 173.

6. Leo Stein, "Notes for Chapters on Matisse and Picasso," c. 1937, quoted in Emily Braun, "Saturday Evenings at the Steins'," in Janet Bishop, Cécile Debray, and Rebecca Rabinow, eds., *The Steins Collect: Matisse, Picasso, and the Parisian Avant-Garde* (San Francisco: San Francisco Museum of Modern Art in association with Yale University Press, New Haven, CT, 2011), 49.

7. William Rubin, "*Boy Leading a Horse*," in Rubin, with Elaine L. Johnson and Riva Castleman, *Picasso in the Collection of The Museum of Modern Art* (New York: The Museum of Modern Art, 1972), 34.

8. Meyer Schapiro, "The Unity of Picasso's Art," 1985, in *The Unity of Picasso's Art* (New York: George Braziller, 2000), 14.

9. Schapiro, "Unity of Picasso's Art," 16.

10. See, for example, Margaret MacNamidhe, "Rose-Period Picasso: Drawing, Effort, and Habit in Modernism," *nonsite.org*, no. 18 (January 2016): nonsite.org/rose-period-picasso/.

11. Kirk Varnedoe, "*Boy Leading a Horse*, Paris, 1905–06," in Varnedoe and Pepe Karmel, eds., *Picasso: Masterworks from The Museum of Modern Art* (New York: The Museum of Modern Art, 1997), 42.

12. Varnedoe, "*Boy Leading a Hose*," 42.

13. See Rabinow, ed., *Cézanne to Picasso: Ambroise Vollard, Patron of the Avant-Garde* (New York: Metropolitan Museum of Art; New Haven, CT: Yale University Press, 2006).

14. Brassaï, *Picasso and Co.*, trans. Francis Price (New York: Doubleday, 1966), 79. On Picasso's fascination with Cézanne and Cézanne's *Bather*, see Elizabeth Cowling, *Picasso: Style and Meaning* (London: Phaidon, 2002), 143–44.

15. Picasso, in Alexander Liberman, "Picasso," *Vogue*, November 1, 1956, 133.

16. See, for example, Patricia Leighten, *Re-Ordering the Universe: Picasso and Anarchism, 1897–1914* (Princeton, NJ: Princeton University Press, 1989), 78.

17. Rubin, "Pablo Picasso: *Boy Leading a Horse*, 1905–06 (cat. 53)," in Rubin and Matthew Armstrong, eds., *The William S. Paley Collection* (New York: The Museum of Modern Art, 1992), 101.

18. Rubin, "*Boy Leading a Horse*," in *Paley Collection*, 102.

19. Picasso, "Statement by Picasso: 1935," in Barr, *Picasso*, 272.

20. Picasso, "Statement," 272.

21. See E. A. Carmean Jr., *Picasso: The Saltimbanques* (Washington, DC: National Gallery of Art, 1980), 55–56.

22. Picasso, "Statement," 272.

23. Picasso, "Statement," 272.

24. Picasso, in Françoise Gilot and Carlton Lake, *Life with Picasso* (New York: McGraw-Hill, 1964), 60.

25. Pierre Cabanne, *Pablo Picasso: His Life and Times*, trans. Harold J. Salemson (New York: William Morrow, 1977), 23.

26. Picasso, "Los cuatro años de Picasso en La Coruña," interview by Antonio D. Olano, in *Picasso e a Coruña* (A Coruña: Axuntamento da Coruña, 1982), 7; translation quoted in McCully, "Chronology," in McCully, ed., *Picasso*, 24.

27. Picasso, letter to an unknown recipient, November 3, 1897, trans. and annotated by Xavier de Salas in "Some Notes on a Letter of Picasso," *Burlington Magazine* 102, no. 692 (November 1960): 483.

28. Brassaï, *Picasso and Co.*, 68.

29. Brassaï, *Picasso and Co.*, 68.

30. On Catalan *modernisme*, see Carmen Belen Lord, "The New Art: Modernisme," in William H. Robinson, Jordi Falgàs, and Lord, *Barcelona and Modernity: Picasso, Gaudí, Miró, Dalí* (Cleveland: Cleveland Museum of Art in association with Yale University Press, New Haven, CT, 2006), 34–41.

31. See Cristina Mendoza and Francesc M. Quílez i Corella, "Nonell and Mani: Two Artists against the Current," in *Barcelona and Modernity*, 125–33.

32. See Theodore Reff, "Harlequins, Saltimbanques, Clowns, and Fools," *Artforum*, October 1971, 30–43.

33. See Molly Dorkin, "Jeune garçon nu à cheval, 1906" and "Kees van Dongen," in McCully, ed., *Pablo Picasso: Jeune garçon nu à cheval, 1906* (London: Simon C. Dickinson, 2014), 10–12, 25–27.

34. Gertrude Stein, *The Autobiography of Alice B. Toklas* (New York: Harcourt, Brace, 1933; reprint, New York: Vintage, 1990), 53.

35. Leo Stein, *Appreciation*, 174.

36. Leo Stein, *Appreciation*, 175. On his denunciation of Cubism, see Leo Stein, "Notes on Pablo Picasso," *New Republic,* April 23, 1924, 229–30.

37. Leo Stein, *Appreciation*, 178.

38. Picasso, "Statement," 272.

39. Gertrude Stein, *Autobiography of Alice B. Toklas*, 6.

40. See Brenda Wineapple, *Sister Brother: Gertrude and Leo Stein* (New York: G. P. Putnam, 1996), 339–92.

41. See Stephanie Barron, ed., *"Degenerate Art": The Fate of the Avant-Garde in Nazi Germany* (Los Angeles: Los Angeles County Museum of Art; New York: Abrams, 1991).

FOR FURTHER READING

Ashton, Dore. *Picasso on Art: A Selection of Views*. New York: Viking, 1972.

Barr, Alfred H., Jr. *Picasso: Fifty Years of His Art*. New York: The Museum of Modern Art, 1946.

Cohen-Solal, Annie. *Picasso the Foreigner: An Artist in France, 1900–1973*. Translated by Sam Taylor. New York: Farrar, Straus and Giroux, 2023.

Cowling, Elizabeth. *Picasso: Style and Meaning*. London: Phaidon, 2002.

Gilot, Françoise, and Carlton Lake. *Life with Picasso*. New York: New York Review Books, 2019. Originally published in 1964 by McGraw-Hill, New York.

McCully, Marilyn, ed. *Picasso: The Early Years, 1892–1906*. Washington, DC: National Gallery of Art, 1997.

Olivier, Fernande. *Loving Picasso: The Private Journal of Fernande Olivier*. Translated by Christine Baker and Michael Raeburn. Foreword and notes by Marilyn McCully. Afterword by John Richardson. New York: Abrams, 2001.

Richardson, John, with Marilyn McCully. *A Life of Picasso*. Vol. 1, *The Prodigy, 1881–1906*. New York: Random House, 1991.

Rubin, William, and Matthew Armstrong, eds. *The William S. Paley Collection*. New York: The Museum of Modern Art, 1992.

Rubin, William, with Elaine L. Johnson and Riva Castleman. *Picasso in the Collection of The Museum of Modern Art*. New York: The Museum of Modern Art, 1972.

Stein, Gertrude. *The Autobiography of Alice B. Toklas*. New York: Vintage, 1990. Originally published in 1933 by Harcourt, Brace, New York.

Varnedoe, Kirk, and Pepe Karmel, eds. *Picasso: Masterworks from The Museum of Modern Art*. New York: The Museum of Modern Art, 1997.

Leadership support for this publication is provided by the Kate W. Cassidy Foundation.

Produced by the Department of Publications
The Museum of Modern Art, New York

Leadership support for this publication is provided by
the Kate W. Cassidy Foundation.

Michelle Kuo, Chief Curator at Large and Publisher
Curtis R. Scott, Associate Publisher
Hannah Kim, Business and Marketing Director
Joseph Mohan, Production Director

Edited by Emily Hall
Series designed by Miko McGinty and Rita Jules
Layout by Amanda Washburn
Production by Matthew Pimm
Image and rights acquisition by Anne Levine
Proofread by Rebecca Roberts
Printed and bound by Offset Yapımevi, Istanbul

This book was typeset in Ideal Sans.
The paper is 150 gsm Magno Satin.

Published by The Museum of Modern Art
11 West 53 Street
New York, NY 10019-5497
www.moma.org

© 2025 The Museum of Modern Art, New York
Certain illustrations are covered by claims to copyright
noted in the Photograph Credits.
All rights reserved

ISBN: 978-1-63345-172-8

Distributed in the United States and Canada by
ARTBOOK | D.A.P.
75 Broad Street, Suite 630
New York, NY 10004
www.artbook.com

Distributed outside the United States and Canada by
Thames & Hudson
6-24 Britannia Street
London WC1X 9JD
www.thamesandhudson.com

Printed and bound in Turkey

PHOTOGRAPH CREDITS

In reproducing the images contained in this
publication, the Museum obtained the permission of
the rights holders whenever possible. If the Museum
could not locate the rights holders, notwithstanding
good-faith efforts, it requests that any contact
information concerning such rights holders be
forwarded so that they may be contacted for future
editions.

All works by Pablo Picasso © 2025 Estate of Pablo
Picasso/Artists Rights Society (ARS), New York

Acr. 20019 © Acropolis Museum Photo Archive,
photograph by S. Mavrommatis, [2012]: p. 14. The Art
Institute of Chicago/Art Resource, New York: p. 22.
Baltimore Museum of Art: p. 27 (both). Photograph
© Barnes Foundation/Bridgeman Images: p. 23.
Bibliothèque nationale de France: p. 38. Bridgeman
Images: p. 24. Granger Historical Picture Archive: p. 10
(left). Kunstmuseum Basel: p. 39. Image © The
Metropolitan Museum of Art, image source Art
Resource, New York: pp. 18, 41. © Museu Nacional
d'Art de Catalunya, Barcelona, 2025: p. 35. Museu
Picasso, Barcelona: pp. 31, 32, 33. Museum Folkwang
Essen – ARTOTHEK: p. 20. Digital Image © 2025 The
Museum of Modern Art, New York, Imaging and Visual
Resources Department: p. 6; photograph by Robert
Gerhardt: cover, pp. 3, 12, 37, inside back cover foldout;
photograph by Thomas Griesel: p. 36; photograph by
Paige Knight: p. 9; photograph by Jonathan Muzikar:
pp. 19, 34; photograph by Martin Parsekian: pp. 4, 25;
photograph by John Wronn: pp. 7, 17. National Gallery
of Art, Washington: pp. 15, 28–29. Photo by Arnold
Newman Properties/Getty Images: p. 4. © RMN–
Grand Palais/Art Resource, New York: p. 13 (both),
back cover. Scala/Art Resource, New York: p. 11. The
Solomon R. Guggenheim Foundation/Art Resource,
New York: p. 16. © Tate, London/Art Resource, New
York: p. 26.

TRUSTEES OF THE MUSEUM OF MODERN ART

Marie-Josée Kravis
Chair

Sarah Arison
President

Sid R. Bass
Mimi Haas
Marlene Hess
Maja Oeri
Vice Chairs

Glenn D. Lowry
Director

Edgar Wachenheim III
Treasurer

James Gara
Assistant Treasurer

James E. Grooms
Secretary

Ronald S. Lauder
Honorary Chairman

Jerry I. Speyer
Chairman Emeritus

Agnes Gund
President Emerita

Ronnie F. Heyman
President Emerita

Wallis Annenberg*
Lin Arison**
Sarah Arison
Alexandre Arnault
Sid R. Bass
Scott Belsky
Lawrence B. Benenson
Leon D. Black
David G. Booth
Clarissa Alcock Bronfman

Patricia Phelps de Cisneros
Steven Cohen
Edith Cooper
Paula Crown
David Dechman
Anne Dias Griffin
Elizabeth Diller**
Glenn Dubin
Lonti Ebers
Joel S. Ehrenkranz
John Elkann
Laurence D. Fink
H.R.H. Duke Franz of Bavaria**
Glenn Fuhrman
Kathleen Fuld
Maurice R. Greenberg**
Agnes Gund
Mimi Haas
Marlene Hess
Ronnie F. Heyman
AC Hudgins
Barbara Jakobson
Pamela Joyner
Jill Kraus
Marie-Josée Kravis
Ronald S. Lauder
Wynton Marsalis**
Khalil Gibran Muhammad
Philip S. Niarchos
James G. Niven
Peter Norton
Daniel S. Och
Maja Oeri
Eyal Ofer
Michael S. Ovitz
Emily Rauh Pulitzer
David Rockefeller, Jr.*
Sharon Percy Rockefeller
Richard Roth
Richard E. Salomon
Ted Sann**
Anna Marie Shapiro
Anna Deavere Smith
Robert Soros
Jerry I. Speyer
Jon Stryker
Daniel Sundheim

Tony Tamer
Steve Tananbaum
Alice M. Tisch
Edgar Wachenheim III
Helen Zell
Xin Zhang

EX OFFICIO

Glenn D. Lowry
Director

Eric Adams
Mayor of the City of New York

Adrienne Adams
*Speaker of the Council of the
City of New York*

Brad Lander
*Comptroller of the City of
New York*

Robert Soros
Chair of the Board of MoMA PS1

Sharon Percy Rockefeller
*President of The International
Council*

Randall Gianopulos and
Margot Ziegler
*Co-Chairs of The Contemporary
Arts Council*

Alvin Hall
Chair of The Black Arts Council

*Life Trustee
**Honorary Trustee